Critical acclaim for

Dog Days in Soho

'[Josh's] memories of Bacon, in particular, are fascinating and reinforce notions of the artist's gambling, benders and whoring as a studied divorce from normality. Richardson's writing is seductively enveloping: the Soho created in his pages is a virtual domain that you wander at will' *Time Out*

'This is a fine study of the melancholy and obsessiveness which become the drunk's world. Richardson understands perfectly how these extraordinary characters work, how self-loathing becomes an addiction, how the only solution to a cracking hangover is a fresh bender. There is violence, jealousy, shame . . . Richardson has done a good job here: melancholy wafts from these pages. And if all biography is a failure, there is nevertheless some glory in this one'
William Leith, *Daily Telegraph*

Breakfast in Brighton

'Richardson is a powerful and companionable storyteller . . . his version of the town is vivid, bright and unashamedly affectionate' Lynne Truss, *The Times*

'As effervescent as Brighton itself' Francis King, *Spectator*

'Brighton's particular genius for unselfconscious eccentricity, its odd mix of the seedy and the decorous, its sheer un-Englishness, was never better portrayed. The swerving, dreamlike narrative suits its subject perfectly'
Paul Mansfield, *Sunday Telegraph*

Nigel Richardson is on the staff of the *Daily Telegraph* and contributes to BBC Radio 4. He lives in south-west London.

FRITH STREET, 1955, BY PETER HURDY (HULTON GETTY)

DOG DAYS IN SOHO

One Man's Adventure in 1950s Bohemia

NIGEL RICHARDSON

PHŒNIX

A PHOENIX PAPERBACK

First published in Great Britain in 2000
by Victor Gollancz
This paperback edition published in 2001
by Phoenix,
an imprint of Orion Books Ltd,
Orion House, 5 Upper St Martin's Lane,
London WC2H 9EA

A CIP catalogue record for this book
is available from the British Library.

ISBN 0 75381 433 1

Printed and bound in Great Britain by
The Guernsey Press Co. Ltd, Guernsey, C.I.

Fare well fare well the sailors
cruising on Friday nights
the fruity streets of Soho
under the gory lights
gunning for beds or brandies
or a middle-aged spectacled queer
the roly poly all night long
the breakfast of a beer

From *In Memory of David Archer*

by George Barker

Acknowledgements

I thank the following for permission to use copyright material: Faber & Faber for the lines from *In Memory of David Archer* by George Barker; Harper Collins for extracts from *Never a Normal Man* by Daniel Farson.

I am indebted to Gordon Avery, Norman Bowler, Michael Law, Virginia Law, former HMS *Ganges* boys Ron Catchpole and George Athroll, and Mike Jacobs for giving of their time and memory. I am most especially grateful to Jean Avery and David Mossman, who allowed me with such grace to appropriate their family; to Reggie Watters, who saw things a long time ago; and to Miren for her seemingly inexhaustible patience and encouragement.

Author's note

To get the business of Josh's name out of the way: I always knew him as Josh Avery, though apparently his real name was Michael Joseph Avery and formerly he had been known as Mick or Mike. Hetta Empson, the wife of poet and critic William Empson, is thought to have been the first person to call him Josh, which might well have been a corruption and contraction of either Joseph or Johnson, the latter being one of the aliases he used while on the run from the navy at the time he met Daniel Farson. There were other aliases, but to keep things simple I will refer to him throughout as Josh, even when describing the time before the name had come into use.

The account that follows is partly fictional. I have tried to make it true to the spirit of time and place, even if it is not accurate in every factual or chronological particular.

For Josh
1932–1993

and for Jean
1929–1999

JOSH AT GREENSANDS (DAVID MOSSMAN)

Chapter 1

The day after they met, Josh Avery and Daniel Farson returned to Soho's moist and maudlin heart. Josh wore Farson's suit, a bit baggy but that was fine, the belt ratcheted tight into his narrow waist. Farson's right cheekbone was swollen and discoloured, his eye was starting to blacken up, but he was in good spirits. 'We're going to the real place this time,' he said. 'The Mandrake is the last resort of Sunday soaks. This place, *this* place is ...' Words fail even the honey-tongued sometimes. '... Well you'll see. And remember what I told you. Don't try too hard, and when in doubt keep your mouth shut and act like you couldn't care less.'

They walked past the basement fire escape that led to the door of the Mandrake, where they had been drinking the day before. They were nearly at the end of Meard Street, where the cobbles open into Dean Street and two stone tablets high up on facing walls bear the same legend, 'Meards Street 1732', commemorating the man who built it and the date it was completed. Josh was looking down, expecting another base-ment entrance. 'This way,' said Farson. 'Here,' and he pushed Josh up a flight of steps, beneath a ponderous stuccoed porch to a studded door with a grille in the middle. Farson reached round Josh and rapped confidently on the door. The grille slid to one side and a face with bloodshot eyes appeared in the aperture. 'Plus one,' said Farson, peering forward over

Josh's shoulder. The face nodded, and the door opened.

Inside, a stream of people waited – for what? – and babbled. Josh gawped at them. The prevailing hues of the post-war years were greys and browns; austerity throbbed like a hangover; people mended and made do. But here was colour and daring, a secret Josh had never guessed at, and, for a fraction of a second, an anger rose in him: the thought that he had stumbled on it by chance, and might never have known. Around him were matelots in uniform (none he recognized, thankfully) and tarts in sequins, old women in turbans and rouge and queeny types in bright waistcoats. Somewhat incongruously, a man in the uniform of an RAF squadron leader stood among them smoking a pipe and tapping one foot softly to a rhythm in his head. Josh heard vowels from both East and West Ends, French-accented English and Italian expletives. There was a miasma of smoke and scent and sweat and, occasionally, a rasping blast of cold, coal-laden city air blew itself out in the small anteroom as the door opened and closed and more bodies tumbled in off the street. Farson caught Josh staring and smiled and raised his eyebrows. 'Simply *the* place to be seen, darling,' he said. 'Some people never make it to the Gargoyle Club. You've found it without even trying.'

The people were waiting for a tiny white sentry box of a lift – the only means of access to the club itself, which occupied the top floor. When their turn came, Farson and Josh squeezed in with the RAF officer. Farson stood beneath the single bulb that lit the lift. In its light his eye and cheekbone looked especially swollen and painful. 'You've been in the wars,' said the RAF officer as the lift creaked upward. 'Still, *per ardua ad astra.*' And he winked at them.

'He always says that,' Farson whispered to Josh as they were getting out, scarcely forbearing to tongue the rim of Josh's ear. They stood at the top of a wide staircase that led down into a ballroom where the squadron leader now disappeared into the thicket of chattering, laughing people. The place seemed huge to Josh, largely an optical illusion as the Gargoyle gained its disconcerting spaciousness from the thousands of squares of mirrored glass decorating the walls. Mirror balls swung from the ceiling. Spotlights picked out a swing band in tuxedos tuning up on a stage. In the shadowy corners of the ballroom couples and groups sat at candlelit tables. The visual effect was dazzling, exhilarating; light and shadow swirled like a speeded-up film of the sky.

'Heard of Matisse?' Farson's voice stuck at an uncomfortable pitch and wobbled above the din. 'Henri?'

Josh nodded, though he hadn't.

'He designed it. Thought it up in a nightmare, I shouldn't wonder. It can be hellish when you've had a few. We should have been here before the war. Then it was really something. It's just my luck, to arrive at the end of things. There was a garden on the roof with pergolas where you could dance by dappled moonlight. All the Bright Young Things were there. See Alec, the band leader?' Farson gestured at the stage. 'He used to play at Maxim's in Juan-les-Pins. Once played "Someone to Watch Over Me" specially for Mrs Simpson. But never ask him about it or he'll bore you to death all night ... Fancy a house special? Pimm's with curaçao, just a dash.'

Josh frowned. 'Beer'll do.'

'Or Dog's Nose? That's another one they do. Beer and gin.'

'Just beer,' said Josh.

Farson bought the drinks – the pattern was already established – and they joined the squadron leader, now installed in a shadowy corner. The squadron leader was talking to a man in a black leather coat, whose large head, as it moved from side to side, seemed to slosh about within the confines of its skin like something viscid in a bag. 'Ah,' said Farson to the

4

man with the sloshing head, drawing up chairs for himself and Josh. 'I thought I might find you here.'

'Dan got's a shiner, haven't you Dan?' said the squadron leader.

'Show mummy,' said the man with the big head. Farson stooped towards the man, who peered forensically at his swollen cheek and blackening eye. 'Mmm, bet that was awfully good fun.'

'The best yet,' said Farson. And now he couldn't resist showing off. 'Francis, meet Mr Alias, Mr Smouldering Spanish Good-Looks, Mr All My Christmases Have Come At Once. He responds to the name Mick.' He turned to Josh. 'Mick. Francis Bacon.'

Bacon scraped back his chair, played his right hand lovingly over his oiled and slicked back hair, and looked Josh up and down with unblinking eyes. Then he turned to Farson and, gripping himself by the throat, became furry and feral, blinking and wobbling furiously before coming out with something in French that managed to sound both arch and profound. Josh said nothing, remained expressionless. In the pockets of his borrowed, baggy suit trousers, he bunched those fists with LOVE and HATE on the knuckles.

Bending low over Bacon, in a voice he thought Josh couldn't hear, Farson continued: 'Look but don't touch.' And then: 'I invented him, darling.' But that was a mistake. Nobody invented Josh. Not I, not Daniel Farson, not a single one of those blithe budgerigars he took to bed or those trembling soaks he took for money and fumbles. Josh pretended he didn't catch what Farson said to Bacon, pretended he was too bewildered by it all, or that the reflected light from all those pieces of mirror dazzled his ears as well as his eyes. But he heard. He was just biding his time.

'And what do *you* do?' asked Bacon, appraising Josh once more. 'Besides the rough and tumble.'

'What doesn't he do, you mean?' lied Farson.

'I'm a painter,' said Josh. 'What about you?'

Josh had landed in Soho the day before, a Sunday afternoon in early 1953; wandered into a pub and had the good fortune to be chatted up by Dan Farson. 'You worked the poofs,' Josh told me, meaning that was what one did. He pitched up in London with no home, no money and no name, and in no time at all had fixed himself up with all three, courtesy of Farson. It wasn't Josh but I who saw this as a pivotal moment in his life. I pointed it out in one of those fabulous conversations we had in the cottage shortly before he died. I can picture him clear as day, sitting on the tea chest from Darjeeling that the television later stood on, his heels swinging against the stencilled slogan on the front: IT PAYS TO BUY GOOD TEA. Outside, the light of a late summer's day was fading; we had already lit a couple of household candles and their light flickered around the deconstructed walls. Josh had rolled and lit a cigarette but, uncharacteristically for him, he got so carried away talking that he left it smouldering on the window ledge. It burned a groove in the ledge which I carefully painted around when I decorated the room after he died, and whenever I looked at that burn-mark afterwards I thought of Josh telling me about his chance meeting with Farson. Everything flowed from that meeting.

The burn-mark was a benchmark: I became Josh's biographer in precisely those moments it took for the cigarette to burn down on the window ledge. Having told me about meeting Farson, his entrée to the world of bohemian Soho, he was already on to Francis Bacon, how it was Bacon who gave him his first painting and decorating job, and I felt the need to stop the flow, throw down some markers. I said something like, 'Hang on a mo, can I stop you there? The Bacon stuff sounds fascinating, but can we just go back to meeting Farson. Would you not say that if he hadn't picked you up by chance, that unpromising-sounding Sunday, your life would have turned out unimaginably differently?' And Josh had agreed readily with this proposition. He had said cheerily – and ironically, in view of the fact that he would be dead within three weeks – that he would have pegged out long before, or spent most of his adult life inside, or on the street, or in the gutter more like.

Josh never tried to rationalize the random events that comprise a life – that's where I came in. He would have said it wasn't good luck, meeting Farson, just as it wasn't bad luck that at the outbreak of war, when he was seven, his father had dumped Josh and his twin elder brothers in an orphanage in Derbyshire because – and Josh was brutally honest about this – big Joe Avery didn't much care for them. No, life for Josh was an entity that he didn't wish to pick over. In those cottage sessions, my promptings, my attempts to see patterns in his life, to understand motivations and marry causes with effects, made him laugh rather uncomfortably, muttering 'I s'pose so', and 'You may well be right.'

By the time I met him his wild days were over. In the early seventies he had met my friend Dave's mother, Jean, at a wedding party in south-west London. It was the first time she had smoked cannabis, she told me, and the room was swirling. He was leaning against the wall looking aloof and desirable, in a Brandoesque sort of way, and she couldn't keep her eyes off him. (He remembered it slightly differently. He was blind drunk, and leaning against the wall to prevent himself slumping to the floor.) They were married six months later, amid confidential predictions of disaster among her friends. And it was true that Josh continued to disappear on occasional benders with his old Hampstead cronies. In order to remove him from temptation Jean sold up in London and moved to the country. She bought a red-brick cottage near the South

Downs in Sussex, called it Greensands after the local sandstone, and filled it up with arty knick-knacks and dogs and cats. Josh swapped his scuffed pub-shufflers for gumboots, looked after the chickens and geese they had bought for the garden, and generally mellowed out. To old London friends who visited, it seemed incredible that this chowder-making, tomato-growing homebody could be the same person as the hellraiser they remembered.

In those days I knew little or nothing of the old Josh. I just loved visiting my mate Dave's house from the nearby boarding school we both attended. The rambling garden, the animals, his willowy, scatty, rather pre-Raphaelite mother, his long-haired 'stepfather' (though both Dave and Josh hated the term) with stubble on his chin and stains on his jeans who liked to talk about sex and swore with insouciance (I think I first heard 'motherfucker' from him). Drink had blurred him at the edges – I remember him looking as if he had just wandered off the edge of a seventies album cover, where he would have been entirely at home standing next to, say, one of the Allman Brothers holding a bottle of bourbon – but he still looked good. I know what you're probably thinking – that he became some sort of father figure to me, but I can assure you that's not the case. I had a perfectly serviceable father of my own in those days, and besides, the whole point about Josh was that he hated authority, was in fact the most complete and benign sort of anarchist I have known. He'd have been horrified at the thought of being anyone's father.

I had a girlfriend for a while, an obstinate girl called Karen who did not believe in intercourse before marriage. I had not known Josh long when Dave invited Karen and me to come over one Saturday afternoon. I have the photograph of the occasion in front of me now: the summer of 1975, a sunny day by the look of it, on the terrace above the lawn; Karen barefoot in a deckchair, side on to the camera, looking extremely pissed off; Jean in sunglasses and fashionable perm; Josh in open-necked white shirt, with more hair than I remembered on top, forking some salad into his mouth from a plate balanced on his knee; behind him on the low wall, pots of geraniums. It pains and amuses me more or less equally when I look at this photograph for I cannot help remembering just why Karen was looking so thunderously displeased. Having known her all of half an hour, Josh had just asked her – as casually and politely as anyone else might enquire after the health of one's grandmother – the following question: 'Hasn't he got his leg over yet then?'

There was a salon quality to Greensands that felt more European than Home Counties. Friends or relatives might pop in while I happened to be there – sexy, bra-less girls that crucial few years older than I was, with nicknames such as the Norfolk Broad or Six-Mile Bottom, divorcées with new, foreign lovers, and, on one memorably surreal occasion, the voice of a television puppet. Everyone seemed more interesting there, things more possible. Obviously this was about the alchemy between Jean and Josh and the kind of people that between them they attracted, but at the time I attributed it also to the place, the cottage itself; the red bricks known as Greensands seemed to have a spirit of their own.

This was partly in my mind when I myself bought a cottage in Sussex a few years ago. The idea of a salon was out of the question. The prospect of lots of clever people circulating about in my cottage saying frightfully clever things made me feel rather sick. But I had rarely been happier than at Greensands, and I reasoned that if I could re-create even a shadow of that old, cocoon-like magic, I would be content. And what better way to start than by getting Josh to paint the place, painting and decorating being his stock in trade?

Joan drove him over the twenty miles or so from Greensands for the last two weeks of August, the old estate car laden with dustsheets, brushes and rollers. I was busy turning one of the bedrooms into an office – building a 'work station' for the computer, with shelving for printer and fax machine (with what innocent enthusiasm I embarked on my bucolic downshifting!). The cottage was still a mess, with plaster off the walls, no beds (I slept on an airbed; Josh, in a fit of machismo, on a tiled floor), electricity disconnected and no cooking facilities.

They were a great few days, made all the more special in retrospect by the fact that it was to be the last time I saw him. There seemed to be something very resigned and wise about Josh by this time, as if a ballast of contentment sat at the heart of his being. He did things slowly, almost ritually – rolling a cigarette, making yet another cup of the instant coffee he drank to combat the booze cravings – paused before he spoke, found all sorts of things wryly amusing. And when he laughed, the skin at the side of either eye broke into a fan-shaped mesh of lines. One evening we sat on the front steps, facing the beech wood on the far side of the valley. He was methodically making a cigarette – the thinnest of Rizla brands, Blue, a sprinkle of Samson tobacco, the wad of white filter – and gazing into the middle distance. The low, golden sun had turned the leaves of the beech trees the most achingly lucent green so the whole valley glowed with life and vigour. Transfixed, we gazed on this scene for a minute or so without speaking. But it was late summer by then, and pretty soon Josh noticed that the scene wasn't quite perfect. He took his half-moon specs – the specs that gave him, in these later years, an improbable professorial air – from his shirt breast-pocket and stared through them intently for a few seconds. 'D'you see?' he said. 'They're turning already, the leaves.' I followed his pointing finger, saw the merest hint of brown in the topmost branches of one of the trees, enough to introduce a note of melancholy where before there had been only demure wonder. Is it fanciful to imagine, in Josh's observation, a premonition of what soon would befall him?

During those few days we worked hard on our respective tasks in the daylight hours, and in the evening convened in the cottage's low, dark sitting room. We made a fire in the fireplace out of the old kitchen units, ate revolting baked beans-and-sausage combinations out of a tin heated on a camping stove, lit candles as the light faded and eased our way back in time and spirit, to Cornwall, the navy, Soho, prison and Hampstead, and all the broken hearts and empty pockets Josh left along the way. I had known him twenty years by this point, but it was only now that I heard these stories and realized he had been there when a glut of arsonists – led by the greatest incendiary of all, Francis Bacon – set fire to mid-century London, and that Josh had danced gleefully in the flames alongside them. I did not feel any urgency about getting these stories down. Josh was only sixty-one and not, apparently, about to pop off, though I do remember resolving that at a later date I would collar him with a tape recorder and record his memories more systematically. But things were about to change.

On his last morning at the cottage, Josh completed the most fiddly bit of the house painting, a large area of wall against which climbed a vigorous red rose whose thorns were as sharp as carpet tacks. In order to get his paintbrush behind the briars, he tied one end of a length of rope to the thickest rose stem, looped the other end over the branch of a nearby tree, and pulled until the entire growth lifted away from the wall sufficiently for him to reach behind without cutting his hands to ribbons. He fixed the rope on the branch with some knot remembered from his navy days, and finished the painting. The tree was a particular favourite of mine, a medlar, a tree of merrie England, whose fruit, some said, resembled in its slimy puckeredness the rectum of a dog. The trunk of the tree was upholstered in emerald moss, its branches twisted into a gnarled picturesqueness. When Josh had finished he was in such a hurry to get his things together before Jean arrived to drive him home that he forgot to untie the rope from the branch.

So Josh left the cottage, having completed the paint job. 'Cheerio,' he said, and in response to my effusive thanks for his tales from Soho: 'No, I'm just flattered that you're interested.' My parting words were about how I would like to resume these conversations on my next visit to Greensands. And on that next occasion, I said, I would come prepared – with notebook and cassette recorder. He said he would like that.

It rained solidly for two weeks after that, washing summer down the grates. It was a Friday and I was on the A24 heading for London when Dave called me on my mobile to tell me Josh had dropped dead of a heart attack earlier that day. Feeling icily calm, I turned straight round and drove back to the cottage in a mental vacuum, arriving in a rainy, blustery, miserable dusk. I didn't notice it immediately. But as I fumbled for the light switch in the kitchen I looked through the window facing the garden and saw a grotesque sight. While I had been out, the medlar tree had keeled over. It lay on its side, its arthritic branches clawing at the cottage wall as if, in its dying, it had reached out for help. The rope that still tied it to the climbing rose lay slack on the grass. All that rain was certainly to blame, but it was essentially the rope that had done for the medlar. The rope had exerted so much pressure that it had pulled the tree over in the waterlogged earth.

There was no funeral service for Josh. He was cremated in the presence of no one bar Jean, Dave and the furnace operator. Half his ashes were scattered in a country lane in Sussex where he liked to walk his dogs. The other half repose in an urn on top of an electric fire in Dave's small flat in

King's Cross. Josh liked to say that he didn't exist – he had no National Insurance number, he never drew state benefit, or indeed paid taxes – and now, shockingly, that almost seemed the case. His estate, his lifetime's accumulation of worldly wealth, was contained in a brown envelope handed to Jean by the mortuary assistant. On the envelope was written: 'Oct 5. Michael Avery. £25.46p + 1 betting slip.' There was so little for me to get to grips with – just a few photos and the stories he had told me in the cottage as he sat on that tea chest.

Now that I was attuned to his heyday, fifties Soho, I realized from the regular newspaper obituaries that others were dying too, those he had known who had also burned themselves out – your early sixties, after all, is not a bad knock if you give your body the kind of hammering that seems to have been more or less obligatory in that crowd. But there was no danger of these people being forgotten, for their dying and deaths had become a minor industry. They were the subjects of stage plays and hagiographies. Their memoirs were published and broadcast. Commentators smiled wryly over the stories of excess. Josh featured in a good proportion of these stories, I noticed, but only ever as a shadow on the margins, a baleful influence, a clownish drunk. They didn't write him out altogether, but they never used his name, these solipsists. Instead they used an old alias, or jumbled two together, or visited on him the casual indignity of leaving him nameless. One photographic caption even described him as 'the naval deserter'.

Here's a typical example, from the obituary of Lady 'Hetta' Empson published in *The Times*. The widow of poet and critic William Empson (like every other student of English literature, I recall failing to read Empson's *Seven Types of Ambiguity* whilst at university), Hetta is described by her obituarist as 'sculptor, political activist, adventurer and socialite':

> Renowned for her statuesque looks and flamboyant gregariousness, Hetta became the cynosure of a large circle and brought a sense of dramatic and often outrageous moment to many social gatherings. Once, at a party, Empson apologized to the writer Charles Osborne for the behaviour of another man. 'There's no need for you to apologize,' said Osborne. 'But there is. He is my wife's lover.' An Empson party was an event.

To put the record straight, the action for which William Empson felt compelled to apologize at his and Hetta's party in Hampstead in 1961 was the bare-knuckle flooring of Charles Osborne; and the man who chinned Osborne – and was indeed Hetta's occasional lover – was Josh Avery. (The trigger for this attack is lost in time, but I remember Josh mentioning the episode to me; he'd thought Osborne was being lofty and patronizing, asking whether Josh had really never heard of some writer or painter or other or was he just affecting ignorance for *faux naif* effect, to get inside some bluestocking's knickers? Josh said this was the kind of thing he had had to put up with all the time, in Hampstead especially.) The point is, if 'an Empson party was an event', it was partly because of Josh, and in particular the sexual forcefield that surrounded him. Got that?

Even when I knew him he still had something of that about him; the embers of his sexual charisma still glowed, and women, often without quite realizing it, still gathered to warm their libidos there; found themselves monopolizing him in conversation, showing off, laughing a little too insistently, edging him into corners of rooms. Or so I witnessed at little gatherings down at Greensands. Josh attributed his undeniably exotic, arresting looks to the fact that one of his grandmothers had been Chinese. It was his little joke, he would narrow his eyes and rock his head inscrutably, but, who knows, perhaps it was true. On the other hand, Daniel Farson, knowing he was originally from Cornwall, liked to think of Josh as a bit of Spanish; a bit of 'Armada' Spanish. In Farson's explanation, the Armada was blown anti-clockwise right round the top of these isles, and on the way down the other side started dropping people off on the western extremities for a spot of cross-pollination with the locals. That was why, to this day, you got such swarthy types in Kerry and Cornwall. Ha! Farson would tell the story in front of Josh, shyly teasing the heavy coils of Josh's blue-black hair where it fell on his collar – and Josh would look meaningfully at his empty glass.

His attraction for homosexual men was obvious. But his aura was felt by straight men too, for there was a thrilling whiff of the wild about Josh that appealed to masculine sensibilities. We men like to believe that somewhere within all of us there is the wolf, just as within every wolf there is the dog, and within the dog the human. Well, Josh was the wolf-man, a leader of wolves among dustbins and jewels. Or so I fancied him to have been.

I can't deny that I felt angry when he died. It's a common enough reaction, so they say. I was angry that in dying he had denied me the benefit of his friendship and company, and of that late blossoming wisdom with which he had seemed to be infused. But my anger was also professional. In dying he had deprived me of full access to the fund of stories about the Golden Age of Soho of which he had allowed me a mere tantalizing glimpse. I was fascinated, in particular, by Francis Bacon. Bacon could lay claim to being the most talented, original and strange Englishman of the twentieth century, yet in this infuriatingly Philistine country few people gave a monkey's about him. Josh had known him, had promised to tell me the story of how and when they got together. What was that story? I would never know. The picture he had sketched for me, in those cottage conversations, was intriguing. The background – that boozy penumbra of pubs and clubs, that reek of smoke in the hair – seemed familiar enough from what I had read of the era; but the foreground and mood were different, darker. I became convinced there was an unspoken truth he had uncovered. He had already dropped hints – but, again, the full-blown version had died with him.

Or had it? It was when I got drunk on my own one night that I asked myself that question. I remembered something Josh had said to me, a variation on that line about the Swinging Sixties: if you could remember them you weren't there. Josh had said that he found it difficult to extricate fact from fantasy when he tried to piece together Soho in the fifties. So much of what he had seen and done had been through the filter of drink, as had been the case with a thousand or more others: a multiplicity of memories osmosed through a thousand pickled cerebral cortices, as many cirrhotic livers and twice as many bloodshot eyes. To paraphrase that poet of the bottle, Malcolm Lowry, in *Under the Volcano*, the poor Sohoites had lost almost all capacity for telling the truth, and their lives had become a quixotic oral fiction. Selective recall, wishful thinking, boastfulness, sphincter-loosening shame, all played a part. Who the hell could say any more what really 'happened'? Example: Josh's and Daniel Farson's respective accounts of their acquaintanceship are so wildly at odds that it is scarcely believable they refer to the same events. In these circumstances – and I was drunk, remember – it came to me in a flash. I would put together my own Golden Age of Soho, borrowing judiciously from that slop-tray of sodden memories until I had a brew as intoxicating as the original. Cheers!

*

If Josh and Farson rarely saw eye to eye on anything, there was one thing they did agree on: Farson was smitten with Ordinary Seaman Michael Avery from the moment he spotted him. The occasion, and they agree on this, too, was a Sunday lunch time in January or February 1953, in a gay pub on the corner of Lower Regent Street. Did Josh know it was a queer hang-out, did he walk in with the express intention of 'working the poofs', as he put it – finding a bed for the night, and some drink for his belly? Or did he extemporize when Farson made his pass? All he could remember was wandering in in his naval greatcoat, the shoulders dark with rain, and Farson, folded on a bar stool with a psychotic hangover, looking up and liking what he saw in the mirror behind the bottles of cheap whisky behind the bar: 'You're all wet! Let me buy you a drink,' he remembered Farson saying to him. 'Please, it's on me.' Perhaps they had another couple – no doubt paid for by Farson – and then Farson suggested they move on for a final drink at a basement club called the Mandrake before last orders at two o'clock. So far it was a strictly casual encounter. They hadn't even exchanged names. Farson was on the look-out for a quick toss-off in a toilet and Josh wanted to get oiled free of charge.

As they stepped from the pub, a copper in a cape came angling from a doorway where he had been sheltering from the rain. The pub door was still swinging when his hand landed on the shoulder of Josh's naval greatcoat. 'Bit of a giveaway, innit son?' Josh spun round and the policeman found himself looking down slightly at a handsome, somewhat cocky-looking young man of twenty or so. The policeman no doubt noted that the young man's face had a bit of a foreign air about it: a complexion more attractively olive and smooth than your average pasty Saxon–Norman genotype; a nose more broad, eyes more feline, slanted, hair heavier, bluer, and now beaded with raindrops. At any rate, suddenly the policeman felt less sure of his ground. 'You *are* Ordinary Seaman Michael Avery of HMS St Austell Bay?' he said.

Knowing Josh, you would have put money on him flooring the copper and legging it. Instead, perhaps picking up the grain of doubt in the policeman's voice, he opened his arms and appealed with a grin to his companion, as if the rather pudgy albinoid bloke he had just left the pub with was an acknowledged arbiter in matters of identity. 'Avery?' he said. 'No, I think you must be mistaken, officer. My name's Mick Johnson.'

'That's right, Mick Johnson,' repeated his new acquaintance, catching on smartly. 'I can gladly vouch for this gentleman's name being Mick Johnson, officer.' And with looks of polite puzzlement the two walked on towards Piccadilly Circus, leaving the policeman narrowing his eyes in the direction of their backs. They walked in collusive silence until they reached Shaftesbury Avenue, when Josh risked a look round then said: 'I don't believe it, the stupid bastard's fucked off. Hah! I owe you for that. I'd buy you a drink but ... Between you and me, I *am* Michael Avery, but I call myself other things to be on the safe side. I'm on the run from the navy.'

As they continued along Shaftesbury Avenue, having shaken off the policeman, Farson risked a hand on the wet shoulder of Josh's greatcoat. 'I felt as if I had crossed a border,' Farson wrote, 'and perhaps it was this element of danger that made me become infatuated.' There were other borders to be crossed. As Farson steered Josh gently into the bottom of Wardour Street and through the moral cordon that has always ringed the heart of Soho, his face registered that frisson of relief you feel when the plane takes off or the ferry slips its mooring – freedom from bloody old England! Here, among the commis chefs and *plongeurs*, the pavement croupiers and extravagant lushes, he was invisible – his great blond beacon of a bonce, his predilection for young men entirely unremarkable amid the alleys and pungencies of England's one and only *quartier latin*.

Farson steered Josh rightward, into a narrow alleyway between tall Georgian townhouses. It wasn't much to look at in daylight, this alley. Cigarette butts and empty packets littered the cobbles. An Italian woman was hanging grubby sheets and bedding out of several top floor windows where they lolled like tongues from the sills. The wind liked to sharpen itself between the old brown-brick walls. On this winter Sunday it cut them as they turned the corner, and Josh kneaded together the lapels of his greatcoat. But at whatever time of day Farson walked this narrow thoroughfare, he always held it in his mind's eye as it looked and felt at night. Night cloaked its grubbiness, exalted the neon and the lascivious. At night Meard Street was where Soho's pulse beat most insistently.

They descended an iron fire escape to a basement door marked MANDRAKE CLUB, and beneath that, in small letters that didn't look as if they entirely believed themselves, LONDON'S ONLY BOHEMIAN RENDEZVOUS. 'Not the most salubrious of establishments,' said Farson, taking the opportunity to caress Josh's neck as he ushered him through the door. 'But it'll do.'

As Josh's eyes adjusted to the cellar-gloom of the Mandrake, he scarcely registered the chess players, the disintegrating newspapers in Cyrillic script, or the sozzled old dear asleep on a bar stool. He was not impressed with the chiaroscuro, the painterly effect of light and shade and slowly billowing smoke wrought by the subterranean light. He remained unmoved by the emigré atmosphere, the cinematic loucheness of the place. What he saw may have been reminiscent of a voguish cold war film starring Stanley Baker in a trenchcoat, but he did not think himself into the frame. He had eyes only for the fat barman, the clock behind the barman's head showing two minutes to two and the bottles of whisky and vodka. He was barely twenty and had eyes only for survival.

Farson acknowledged the barman, 'Boris', and ordered two doubles each. They took a table. Josh walloped the first in one, looked steadily at Farson, head on one side, narrowed his eyes, and held his gaze until Farson felt the dark, smoky surroundings retreat like stage props on casters – the two fat men playing chess, the drunk old lady now rattling a tin with coppers in it and saying forlornly, 'M'deah, I say . . .', the tatty Russian newspapers – and his prick begin to stiffen. Josh looked at his knuckles beneath the table, brought up his fists and laid them on the table in front of Farson so the knuckles were legible, should Farson happen to look. LOVE or HATE, which was it to be? He decided to turn on his smile, guaranteed to dazzle. 'That was a close one,' he said, 'with the copper. Thanks and', he nodded at his glass, 'thanks for this.'

'Glad to be of help,' said Farson, holding Josh's gaze. 'Here's to you. The one that got away.' He raised his glass. 'Whatever your name is – you've got me all confused!'

And Josh smiled brighter than ever, the widening grin cracking the panes of his cheeks. 'Call me Mick,' he said.

'Mick. Daniel,' said Farson, blinded by the smile. 'Dan.' They clinked tumblers. Farson held out his free hand, which Josh shook limply across the table. A wet fish handshake, you might call it, or limp lettuce, but Farson, even in the first throes of his infatuation, really should have taken it as a warning sign: the handshake not of a weakling but of someone who couldn't be bothered with the business of handshakes in the first place. 'Shouldn't you be lying low?'

Josh shrugged, looked about him. The basement was low-lit. He felt the damp of it. One of the chess players adjusted his seating position and farted, briefly and comically, like a pop gun. 'I am,' said Josh.

Farson laughed. 'We couldn't get much lower.'

'I wouldn't reckon on that.'

Farson had left his hand on the table between them. Now he leant over again, brushed droplets of rain from Josh's serge coat. 'Look at you, you're all wet. You need to dry off somewhere. Got somewhere to stay?'

'I thought I had. It fell through,' said Josh.

'That's handy,' said Farson. 'If you're looking for somewhere to hide out for a while...'

'I'm not hiding,' said Josh.

'Well,' said Farson, 'it isn't much, but what I have is yours. If you're interested.'

'I might be,' said Josh. 'What've you got?'

'A flat in Beauchamp Place.' Josh must have frowned, not knowing London then, for Farson added: 'Not too far. We'll have you dried off and warmed up in no time. It's more like one room actually. But it's – cosy. And safe.'

'Got a bath?' said Josh. 'I could do with a bath. Slow and hot.'

'It can be arranged,' said Farson. 'If you're discreet. You look the discreet type.'

'Oh I am,' said Josh. 'You'd never know I was there.'

'Just as well,' said Farson. He dropped his voice to a whisper. ''Cos we'll have to walk on tippity toes.' And, half drunk, he risked adding an endearment: 'Darling.'

JOSH IN THE NAVY

Chapter 2

On his butcher's bike, feet off the pedals and turned up like Aladdin's slippers, the errand boy freewheels down the hill into the centre of Liskeard. 'There he goes,' says the old, bearded tobacconist, catching a flash of bike and rider through his pipe-strewn window. 'Bang on time. The boy what thinks he's a dog.' And though there is no one in the shop, and he is talking to himself, the tobacconist laughs wheezily at his own observation. 'He'll start barkin' soon, 'stead of talkin', that boy.'

Wind parts the errand boy's black hair as he whizzes downhill. The hair is so thick that a mere breeze will scarcely ruffle it, but the boy has got a speed on this morning, smoothing his torso along the top of the bike, blinking back the protective tears that spring to his eyes. The wind roars in his ears, the morning sun falls on the nape of his neck and joy, like a piece of origami, unfolds in the boy's head. For it is summer and the war is over, he is back in Cornwall after six years in an orphanage, and he has his dogs.

They are waiting, as usual, the retriever, the three Heinz 57 varieties, the Welsh collie who looks by turns sad and happy, and the two Alsatians. He wonders how they get there. Do they swagger through the town like lads on a night out, stopping off at each other's houses? Or do they slink there one by one? But they are always at the butcher's when he arrives, standing outside, good as gold. In fact they have become a draw. Shopkeepers – excepting the shop-bound tobacconist – come out to watch the daily gathering. They grin across the thoroughfare at one another, arms crossed on their aprons or overalls, waiting for the best bit, the arrival of the boy they have christened Dogboy. For when Dogboy arrives, the dogs send up a tremendous barking in greeting and the shopkeepers, finding this unaccountably and unfailingly hilarious, laugh their smocks off.

A fourteen-year-old Josh steers through this cheering funnel of man and beast and props his bike between the grocer's and the butcher's. He is a shortish, spindly, bow-legged boy, but, even at this age, there is something wiry and implacable in his demeanour. And his face! His face is both exquisite and lopsided, the face of a cherub who squints through keyholes and sees things that cherubs should never see. Cycling every day in the sun and wind has polished his features till they glow like an apple, though, at this moment, it's not just the bicycling that makes Josh glow. He holds down his hands to quell the barking, tumbling mass of fur around him, and the dogs quieten instantly. This is the final bit of entertainment, watching the way Dogboy can command his dogs, and now the shopkeepers, with a wave to Josh, go back to their business.

He goes into the shop. The bell on the door rings. 'Mornin' Mister Brayne.'

'Mornin' Michael,' says Butcher Brayne. He presents Josh with a series of parcels wrapped neatly in newspaper – 'Them's your errands,' he says – and a bag of bones: 'And them's your bones.' And as Josh is half-way out of the door Butcher Brayne adds what he always adds: 'Don't go mixing 'em up now, boy.'

And Josh replies what he always replies: 'I wouldn't do that now, Mister Brayne.'

Outside, Josh props the bag of bones on the window ledge

and puts the parcels in the voluminous wicker basket which is suspended by two leather straps from the handlebars of his bike. He takes his time, checking the list of addresses he has also been given and arranging the parcels in the order in which he will deliver them. The dogs, meanwhile, are watching his every move, heads and eyes following his hands, with the occasional, beseeching glance at the bones on the window ledge. Josh knows the dogs are watching him, willing him to finish what he is doing with the parcels and get on with distributing the bones. He enjoys feeling their rapt attention, without ever looking directly at them. If he lifts a parcel in the air he sees, on the edge of his vision, seven snouts raised in unison; if, keeping it in the air, he moves the parcel to the right, the snouts tilt right, and so on. He marvels at the dogs' self-restraint. Though they are bursting to get at the bones, though their bodies bulge with suppressed barks and whines and their eyes are luminous with longing, they scarcely move or make a noise.

He picks up the bag and walks round the corner into a cobbled alleyway followed by the dogs. The bones clatter in the bag: *thock, thock.* Josh pulls out the first, a ball joint, smooth-globed, membranous. 'Here.' There is an order for giving out the bones: the first to the mongrel with the tan patch over his eye, the second to the thicker coated of the Alsatians, and so on, down to the smallest of the mongrels. They await patiently their turns. As soon as they receive their bones they find a patch of cobbles well away from any other dog and settle down to licking and gnawing. Now they are as happy as a dog can be, and as dogs seem to have an extraordinary capacity for uncomplicated happiness, that is probably very happy indeed.

Josh is also happy. Now he will leave the dogs, so engrossed in their bones they will not notice him go. He will bicycle about on his errands – mornings for the butcher's, afternoons for the grocer's – and look forward to seeing the dogs again the next morning. This routine started back in the winter, which already seems impossibly long ago, shortly after he came back from the orphanage. One of the dogs just happened to be hanging about as he arrived at the butcher's for work, and he asked Butcher Brayne if he could give it a bone. It has evolved into something that now occupies much of Josh's young world, something that he can set his clock by, as it were. But routine, whilst comforting, is treacherous. One day, routine will let you down. And, on this bright and breezy summer's morning, it proceeds to do so.

As usual, he leaves the dogs to it. He exits the alley, picks up his bike and sets off on his first call of the day, a widow in Moorswater. It's the shadow he sees first. Pedalling west out of town, he is riding on the edge of his own shadow when he notices another shape, another shadow, behind it. He swivels in his saddle to see that he is being followed by the mongrel with the eyepatch, the one who always gets his bone first. Josh halts in a squeaking of brakes. The mongrel jumps up and licks him. 'No,' says Josh. He pushes the dog down. 'Bad dog.' But his heart isn't in this admonishment and, encouraged by the sound of his master's voice, the mongrel continues to wag his tail. Josh points back the way they have come. 'Go on,' he says. 'Go back.' But, having got this far, the mongrel has no intention of returning.

Josh tries again. He puts down the bike and squats down by the mongrel. Putting his mouth to the dog's velvety ear flap he enunciates 'Go home' and points back along the road. As he follows the line of his finger he sees something that makes him break out in a sweat. Blobs on the horizon, getting bigger: furry blobs in the middle of the road; dogs coming towards him at a trot down the middle of the road, tails a-bob like markers in a swell. And behind them, following at fractionally less than the speed of a dog trot, the town's coal lorry.

Josh stands in the middle of the road and feebly, knowing it is hopeless, tries to wave the dogs back, to return the devotion of the dogs to the bottle he has uncorked. The dogs take his gestures as greetings and grow delirious with barking, bounding pleasure as they reach him. Josh dashes to the side of the road so that the dogs will clear a path for the lorry. The driver leans from his cab as he passes. 'Keep your bloody dogs under control, boy, or they'll be dealt with next time,' he yells.

'They're not my dogs!' replies Josh, but his voice is drowned by the crunch of the lorry's gears. What is to be done with the dogs? He can't take them to their owners because he doesn't know who they belong to. Taking them to his own house is out of the question, just thinking what his father would do terrifies him. In the end he decides he will have to outpace them, hope they won't be able to keep up with his bike and will eventually lose interest and head back into town. So it is that Josh rises warily to his feet and mounts his bike. The dogs bark. He, and they, set off towards Moorswater, on one of those long and rolling country roads that is both epic and homely; between hedgerows of hawthorn and verges of cow parsley, past lonely crossroads and sunlit fields of shorn sheep. The warmth of the sun is on his neck and jaw, the wind blows through that hair.

The dogs, in the event, find it easy to keep up. They yap at his circulating feet on the pedals. They dice with the spokes, never quite getting their neck fur caught in them. And Dogboy is happy, after all, that they have followed even though, in his heart of hearts, he knows they are all heading for disaster. This is the dream that buoys Josh up most nights, in which, defying the future, he bicycles forever with the dogs in tow.

*

It was Josh's elder brother, Gordon, who told me the Dogboy story. Gordon still lived in Liskeard. I drove down there to see him, feeling uneasy. For all I knew, he might take exception to my excavating his dead brother's life; might throw me out, or worse. I needn't have worried. He was a very quiet chap, which you might well be too if you had had what is now referred to as a Near Death Experience. I said Gordon still lived in Liskeard, but it would be more accurate to say he had returned there, after serving, like his twin brother Cyril (known as Swiz), in the RAF. In the mid-1950s, so Gordon told me – the first thing he told me, in fact – he was instructing National Service recruits at a base at Bridgnorth, Shropshire when he suffered a brain haemorrhage. He bent down to light the fire in the married quarters he and his first wife had just moved into, and woke up several days later in hospital in London. In between, a priest had administered the Last Rites, a fact of which Gordon seemed to be rather proud. He had a thin voice and a pallor about him, an air of not being quite of this world, that made sense when you knew about his brush with death; as if, having straddled that threshold, he could never wholly return.

It was certainly strange to meet Josh's brother, and to look in vain for sibling similarities. He was a stooped man with a look of perpetual surprise in his eyes and a soft but marked Cornish accent. The exotic slant of Josh's features was entirely absent; he looked and sounded nothing like his little brother. Josh had been convinced they had had different fathers, which might explain the Chinese grandmother and would certainly account for the powerful antipathy felt by Joe Avery towards his youngest 'son'. Gordon wouldn't be drawn on the question of the Chinese grandmother. Three times I asked him and three times he affected not to hear properly, pretending he thought I was asking whether Josh had ever had any Chinese *girlfriends*. But he was more forthcoming about their mother and father.

Now we got stuck into what Holden Caulfield calls 'all that David Copperfield kind of crap'. Perhaps bestowing some retrospective respectability, Gordon said his father Joe had worked as a lorry driver for the railways. (Josh remembered him as a coalman and, in the summer, occasional bare-knuckle fairground fighter who also did painting and decorating when money was tight.) Their mother was from a fairground dynasty in Plymouth called Tommy Whitelakes. Gordon described her as 'a very good looking woman, a proper model-type, you know'. They lived first in Plymouth, where Josh was born in September 1932. Joe moved the family to Liskeard after some unspecified trouble with his wife in Plymouth – probably to do with a man – but the marriage continued to be rocky. Josh's mother quickly became known as the most glamorous woman in Liskeard, a status which, according to Gordon, went to her head. He remembered terrible fights between his parents over real or imagined infidelities during which they would wrestle with each other on the kitchen floor.

When Josh was five, his parents were divorced. The grounds were probably her adultery, as the father was given custody of the three children and forbade their mother from ever contacting them. Josh did not see his mother again. Two years later the Second World War started, which gave Joe Avery the excuse to dump his kids in an orphanage. He found one that would take them in Derbyshire and they remained there for the duration of the war. Gordon said the regime was spartan but not especially cruel for its day, except on one occasion. In 1940 or 1941 the army requisitioned part of the orphanage, and it was decided to move all boys under the age of eleven to another boys' home twenty miles away. This meant that Josh, then eight or nine, was to be split up from his twin elder brothers. The three had formed a close unit;

'When you picked on one Avery, you picked on three,' Gordon remembered. They pleaded with the principal for an exception to be made in Josh's case, for him to be allowed to stay behind. But the system was inflexible. Josh had to go.

Josh's reaction to this (as described by Gordon) was significant, to my mind. As soon as he got to his new orphanage he did a bunk, the first of many in his life. But he wasn't stupid enough to make his way back to the old orphanage where his brothers remained. This would have been a futile gesture as he would merely have been punished and returned whence he came. What he did was to put the wind up the authorities good and proper by disappearing: an eight-year-old boy with no means of support, at the mercy of the elements, of old pit shafts and perverts, disappears off the face of the earth! After three days, he was found in a railway carriage shunted into a siding outside Derby station. He had assembled a survival kit of stolen food and blankets and could have gone on for several more days. But he had made his point. He was returned to his brothers' orphanage.

At the end of the war their father was obliged to take the boys back. During their six years in Derbyshire, Joe Avery had sent them not a single Christmas card or letter, let alone food or gifts. They were taken from the orphanage to Derby railway station and left on the platform with travel vouchers and a notice hanging round young Josh's neck: 'Please make sure these boys get to Liskeard, Cornwall.' After a tortuous nine-hour rail journey, they got off at Liskeard to find no one waiting for them on the platform. In fact Joe was waiting outside, pacing up and down smoking and looking at his watch. He didn't recognize them and they didn't recognize him. 'You the Avery boys?' he asked gruffly when they shuffled out. 'Come wi' me.' It was winter then. By the spring Josh had a job as an errand boy and was briefly happy with the wind in his hair and the dogs to look after. But Joe Avery was about to put a stop to that.

Loving dogs ran in the family, Gordon said. To illustrate this he told the story of his own dog, a diabetic labrador, whom he had nursed through blindness and incontinence, taking urine samples (how, exactly? He didn't go into detail and I didn't press him) and administering insulin injections. A framed photograph of this plucky mutt held pride of place on the television set. 'He ripped the heart out of me when he died,' he said. But Josh's devotion to dogs was unmatched. By the age of fourteen, he had lost a mother and been abandoned by his father, or the man who passed for his father. His twin elder brothers had each other, but he was on his own. Those dogs in Liskeard who appointed him their pack leader in the spring of 1946 were the first creatures, bar Gordon and Swiz, he could trust. The first creatures who loved him, and with a boundless and worshipful passion.

Gordon recalled the unutterable delight with which Josh greeted each new day when he knew he had the dogs to go to. It more than made up for the routine neglect and mistreatment he suffered at home at the hands of his father. Big Joe Avery, whom Gordon described several times, with a withering shake of the head, as 'a hard man', was evidently not fit to bring up children. He evinced very little interest in Gordon and Swiz, except in respect of their punctuality at mealtimes and the shortness of their hair, but for Josh he reserved a vigilant sadism. If he got wind that Josh liked anything he would take it away or otherwise destroy it. Josh's football card album was an extravagance the tight household budget could not sustain, and was burnt on the bonfire. His catapult was confiscated, his clockwork train given away because Big Joe said Josh was too old for it: 'You're a working man now, for God's sake.'

Josh learned the art of concealment, especially where the

dogs were concerned. It would have been bad enough for his father to find out he gave strange dogs bones every morning, but when they started following him on his errands he knew the consequences would be dire if Big Joe got wind. But it wasn't just the physical chastisement Josh feared. What he really couldn't bear was the thought of having the dogs taken away from him. At the same time he knew it was only a matter of time before his father found out, for Josh was becoming something of a celebrity on the streets of Liskeard: 'Dogboy, the boy what thinks he's a dog.'

Gordon was there when it happened, when Big Joe found out. He and Josh were in the passageway, about to slip out the back way, when a knock came on the front door one Saturday morning. Their father answered it in his vest. 'Is this where Mick, the errand boy, lives?', said a man's voice. 'He's been putting ideas in my dog's head.' Josh and Gordon froze. Gordon pulled a face at Josh. 'He won't eat what we give him no more,' continued the voice. 'It ain't good enough, what we give him, no more. Not since your boy's been feeding him from the butcher's. And then he's gallivanting off half the day, chasing your boy's bike half-way round blimmin' Cornwall.'

'Is this right, our Mick?' Joe Avery turned from the stranger at the door and bellowed back along the hallway. 'You been putting ideas in this man's dog's head?' Gordon scarpered out into the back yard. Joe beckoned Josh to the front door, tugged him by the collar out on to the step. Josh could smell Joe Avery's armpits as he passed beneath his father's arms.

Just off the front step, but near enough for a fine spray of spittle to wet Josh's temple when he spoke, stood a balding man in fuzzy sideboards, his cheeks the high colour of virtuous indignation; by his side an Alsatian dog whose head the man kept semi-averted by means of a rope noose held as tight as it would go without actually throttling the animal. The dog was one of the Alsatians that Josh had been feeding. It recognized its benefactor and began to wag its tail and roll its shoulders in a swoon of doggy delight. 'Ge' down,' shouted the man. He slapped the dog on the snout and twisted the rope, tightening the noose and coercing the dog's head into a yet more awkward position so it was looking at Josh sideways with the white crescents of its eyes, from an unnaturally still head. With occasional, sneering nods down at Josh, the man at the door proceeded to fill in the details of the Dogboy story, as related to him that morning by the tobacconist. 'You're blimmin' barmy, boy,' he concluded, 'carrying on with dogs like that. You'll cause a bad accident one day, 'part from anything.'

'Just how many dogs you carrying on with?' demanded Joe.

'Ooh, least half-a-do'en I should think,' said the man. 'Least.'

'Sshh,' said Joe, 'I want to hear it from the boy.'

Josh shrugged. 'About four – seven,' he admitted.

'Seven!' bellowed his father. 'You're carrying on with seven dogs! Taking advantage of seven dogs! You want your head examining, boy.'

'I'm telling you,' said the man, 'I want it stopping.'

'D'you hear him?' said Joe. 'I catch you near any of them dogs again, you'll be for it.' And he looked meaningfully at his bunched fist. 'We should have left you in that orphanage, eh Mick? We don't like funny sods round here.'

'If you're so keen on my dog, you can blimmin' well look after him yourself,' said the man, scenting victory.

'All right,' said Josh. 'I will. I'll have him if you like.'

'What did you say?' said Joe. 'We'll not have no dogs in this house.'

'Now he's trying to take my dog away from me!' said the man. 'I'm telling you, you just keep well away from my dog, 'cos if you so much as look at him, I'll have him put down.'

The man looked pleased to have thought of this. He looked down at his dog, twisted the rope even tighter, and lifted the front of the animal off the ground by its neck. The body of the animal went stiff. It hopped forward on its back legs, the claws scraping on the path, as it tried to ease the pressure on its neck. In response, the man lifted the rope a fraction higher. The dog's eyes bulged.

Josh lunged for the dog. Joe Avery batted him sideways with the back of his hand and Josh felt the hot abrasion of brick on the rim of his ear as he fell, and heard the strangled yelp of the dog. 'D'you hear what the gentleman says?' said Joe. ''Cos next thing you know, there'll be a dead 'un. And when there is, we'll know who to blame, eh Mick?'

For strapping Joe Avery, who took on all-comers at west-country spring fairs, having Josh around must have been like wearing a pair of permanent cuckold's horns. Had his bold and beautiful slattern of a wife gone with some slanty-eyed riff-raff down on the Devonport docks, some bandy-legged bastard from Shanghai or Kowloon, because Big Joe, even Big Joe, wasn't virile enough for her? She could take on the world and it wouldn't be enough for her, and Josh – of the unmistakably foreign looks – was her appetite in human form. Josh's stay in Liskeard following his return from the orphanage became harder and harder to bear as Joe Avery systematically stripped him of all comfort – even, with those heavy fists, his blossoming looks. If Josh's biological father really was a sailor, as seems plausible, there is symmetry in the fact that Josh bunked off to join the navy as soon as he was old enough – fifteen and a quarter – though in truth 'bunking off' is a bit strong, as no subterfuge was required. Joe was happy to see the back of him.

In late 1947 or early 1948, Josh enlisted as a boy seaman at a training base in Suffolk called HMS Ganges. Here he found himself one among two thousand raw recruits – known as nozzers – being trained up to do the dirty and menial work aboard Her Majesty's fleet. He wore his blue-jean collar and white cap, the gold G of Ganges directly above the bridge of his nose, and quickly absorbed the only naval precepts he needed to know: 'If it moves, salute it; if it's stationary, paint or polish it.' He stripped to the waist to scrub his hammock with carbolic and water and elbow grease; he polished dustbins to a glittery sheen with metal polish; he even buffed up the soles of his boots. And then, he told Gordon, an instructor would come along wearing white gloves and find the only speck of dust in Suffolk, the merest smudge on the tip of his gloved forefinger, to crucify him with. 'You Boy! Name?'

'Avery, Sir.'

'Well, Boy Seaman Avery, answer me this. Has an Ay-rab taken a shit in this bowl? 'Cos that's what it looks like, you filthy little swine. Clean it again. And again. Use your tongue if you have to, but get it *clean.*'

Gordon told me what he knew of Josh's life at Ganges and his subsequent naval career. Then he conjured a road atlas from the side of his armchair to show me where Ganges had been. 'Blow me,' he said. 'It's still marked.' There it was in red letters, on the tip of a spit of land created by the estuaries of the Orwell and the Stour: HMS Ganges. Facing it across the Siamese river mouth were the ports of Harwich and Felixstowe.

I had the bit between my teeth now. I said goodbye to Gordon and his wife (Gordon was fading fast after his exertions in bringing the past to life), and decided to drive overnight, about as far as you can go, laterally, in England, from Cornwall to Suffolk.

I like driving at night – the cosiness and anonymity of it. Nobody knows where you are, nobody can even see you, and the infinitely complex and exhausting world is reduced to a ribbon of silver tarmac and a corridor of silhouettes. And as I drove, with the road largely to myself, I was reminded of a car journey I had taken a few weeks after Josh's death.

Still suffering his loss, still with him near the front of my mind, I was driving through Norfolk on one of those country roads so empty, flat and straight that you can safely look around you for seconds at a time. I had come from an old manor house of Elizabethan vintage which stood next to a church with an ancient, spreading yew in the churchyard. There was no sign of human habitation for miles around these buildings, for this had been a plague village. The hovels of the peasants had been abandoned and had rotted away centuries ago. No doubt an aerial photograph would reveal the ghostly contours of streets around the two structures that had been built to last forever, the manor house and church. The house was on the market for £400,000, an excellent price considering the amount of land and outbuildings, but the owners had had trouble selling it. Why was this the case? I had gone to find out.

This is what I did – write about property matters for a Sunday broadsheet paper, and, though I say so myself, in a manner that revolutionized this hitherto rather dreamy branchline of national newspaper journalism. I used to do all sorts of hack work – travel, restaurants, even (God help me) celeb. interviews – but I found myself returning with a sense of relief to property. To put it simply, property didn't involve having to meet people head on, except for the predictable breed of estate agents and I learned to cope with their sharp suits and blunt brains. With property you are dealing with stone and brick and timber; things that cannot answer back, stare you out, or flirt. Yet these inanimate things have probably witnessed more, and stranger, human goings on than you or I can imagine. And this is what I proved good at – capturing the *genius loci*, peopling empty rooms with all sorts of human life and conflict. I liked to think that people read my articles for the ghosts as much as for the fabric of a place. I could even hear voices if the mood took me.

So I was driving along, wondering just why it might be that some monied gent with a yen for feudalism hadn't yet snapped up the Norfolk manor house, and deciding that a distinct pall of melancholy covered the place, the historic link with the plague being too neat to ignore, when I remember noting with surprise that in the space of ten minutes I had seen three cars with American number plates. I then realized that my route – on to Lincolnshire, to check out a mildewed rectory – was taking me past the USAF airbase at Lakenheath. As well as the gas guzzling cars and unfamiliar licence plates, there were roadside diners, flags and Jeep dealerships that had turned this corner of the Suffolk–Norfolk border into a passable mock-up of small-town America. Thus reassured, I returned to my discursive thoughts on the plague, and the extent to which a place can be imbued with the events that happened there. Was it true, for instance, that birdsong is never heard at Belsen or Dachau?

When I first saw the car coming the other way I assumed I had simply misjudged its position and speed. I had been gazing wildly around; at the big flatland sky, rococo with clouds; half-tiled cottages; strange blokes at the side of the road doing apparently nothing who stare back with expressionless eyes. Then my eyes swung forwards again and there was the car: growing larger with improbable speed in my windscreen and – more to the point – driving on the wrong side of the road, on my side; on a collision course.

What followed is only expressible in cliché. Time slowed down; things went into slow motion. I remember seeing the American radiator grille coming on to me; the headlights flashing; I recall furiously pressing the end of the steering wheel stem to sound the horn, and lifting it to flash the brights; I remember having enough time to register that there was not enough time to feel fear. I held my nerve, thank God, for the other car swerved into the oncoming lane just in time, and our wing mirrors screamed past each other at a closing speed of 160m.p.h. or so. I saw the other driver flash by, looking his apologies through big frightened eyes, and I understood what had happened. He was a black American serviceman, had probably been over here less than a week. He had been lulled, like me, by the straight, empty road, until he was back in East Texas or wherever; with no other cars about, he had simply reverted to driving on the right. The following night I had a nightmare in which the frightened face of the serviceman, so far from home, dissolved into Josh's face. It was so weird that in the midst of my terror, I remember wanting to laugh – apart from anything, Josh didn't drive, for God's sake!

My next assignment, a week after that, happened to be in the heart of Soho. One of those lovely old Georgian houses, with many original features (and a consequent Grade II* listing), had come on the market in Meard Street. Meard Street had immediately rung a bell. Hadn't Josh mentioned this narrow, partly cobbled thoroughfare that links Wardour and Dean Streets? A flick back through the notes I was beginning to keep confirmed that it had been home to two of Josh's regular hangouts, the Mandrake and the Gargoyle, which made this assignment rather poignant. Number nine, built on three floors with basement and garret, stands half-way along Meard Street on the southern side. The asking price, in excess of £1.2 million, reflected the rarity with which such properties become available. Though it is flat-fronted, it stands proud of the houses to the east, which gives it a view down Meard Street to Dean Street and lets plenty of light into the first floor drawing room and main bedroom above.

'The restless and mischievous spirits of Soho past haunt both the house and the street,' I wrote with glee in the resulting article. For in the course of my researches, I had made some felicitous discoveries.

An early occupant of number nine was an architectural designer and landscape gardener called Batty Langley. Langley ran an academy of draughtsmanship in the house, produced many 'pattern books' of architectural drawings which enabled Georgian stonemasons to dispense with the wearisome need for architects, and in general operated as a jobbing purveyor of instant Arcadia to the gentry, advertising his proficiency in the design of 'grottos, cascades, caves, temples, pavilions and other rural buildings of pleasure'. Langley died in 1751, and seven years later number nine Meard Street opened its robustly panelled and heavily knockered door to a woman of singular elan.

Elizabeth Flint, from what I could find out, was the proto-type for any number of charming but dodgy Soho denizens since. Dr Johnson, who drank at the Turk's Head Tavern in nearby Gerrard Street, acknowledged that Betty Flint lived in 'genteel lodgings' at Meard Street. She was nevertheless, he said, a 'slut and drunkard, occasionally a whore and thief'. Betty had a characteristically Soho way with her; she owned a spinet, a sort of small harpsichord, and though she could not play it, said Johnson, 'she put herself in fine attitudes and drummed'. On one occasion, after being sentenced to jail for theft, she rode to prison in a sedan chair with her foot-boy walking before her.

My idea was to set the scene in the article by invoking Soho's Golden Age – Meard Street had been the location of one of London's most famous and glittering nightclubs, the Gargoyle Club, where Jean-Paul Sartre got pissed, Tallulah Bankhead danced and Francis Bacon was entranced by the gossip; next door to it, in the basement Mandrake Club,

Russian emigrés played chess and George Melly played jazz – and cover the obligatory stuff about the house's original features (panelling, cornices, dado rails, moulded architraves, scrolls on the staircase, marble fireplaces on the first floor, Bath-stone fireplaces on the second, etc. etc.). Then I would go to town on Betty Flint. That was the idea. But something rather strange happened.

The estate agent, a square-set woman who put me in mind of furniture, had let me into the house and left me there for half an hour. I poked around for a bit, making notes, then settled in the first-floor drawing room where Betty Flint probably would have failed to play her spinet. To me, empty, newly refurbished old houses were like a vacuum. Into them, if one was patient, rushed ghosts. I trod softly across the freshly planed and stained floorboards, I inhaled the smell of the 'traditional range' paint. I listened to the sound of the city, like a wave always about to break. I was waiting for the ghost of Betty Flint: the rustle of her skirts as she made her entrance; the smell of her face powder; the clearing of her throat; the commencement of her comical thumping of her spinet. I was waiting for Betty Flint, but I got another ghost instead.

It was the soft hissing of water that alerted me. The estate agent had been banging on about how sensitively the 'services', the water, central heating and drainage pipes, had been introduced. 'Bringing the place bang up to date while retaining the integrity of the period features, that was the challenge. And as you can see, ha ha, the challenge was met,' as she put it in her jolly saleswoman's patter. I heard the sound of escaping water and immediately thought that somewhere, behind an original panel or piece of scroll-work, a sensitively introduced pipe had sprung a leak. I followed my ear, turning this way and that, until I found myself by the side window that faced east, back along Meard Street to Dean Street.

Having listened carefully at the panelling that surrounded the window, and pulled out the concertinaed shutters to check behind them, I realized that the sound, which had now subsided and was barely audible, was coming from outside. I looked down the cobbled street. There was nothing unusual. A small van was parked on double yellows with its tailgate yawning. A man was unloading large packets of paper into a print workshop, waddling comically as he lugged the reams at crotch level. Another man in a hard hat and collar-and-tie was standing on the tiptoes of his Wellingtons to scan the chimneypots at the far end of the street. The sound of someone clearing his throat, then spitting, came so astonishingly loud that I jumped, imagining for a split second I was not, after all, alone in the room. I pressed my face to the window and looked down, and there, in the angle made by the railings of number seven and the side of number nine, a young man was urinating. I looked directly on to the crown of his head, watching the way his black hair grew in a whorl from the centre. His head was bowed in happy absorption over the task in hand. He stood facing the houses, and he had the relaxed, slightly bendy legged stance of the professional public urinator. Around his feet the urine flowed, finding its level and meandering off eastward in rivulets among the cobbles – what looked like a bucket's worth, foaming up like dirty car-wash on a driveway.

It could have been something to do with the way the man had been standing. Down in Sussex, Josh would stand like that when he urinated, which he did copiously and often because, he said, his plumbing was shot after all that booze. He would break off from what he was doing, some gardening task, or throwing sticks for the dogs, turn round, bend his legs so he bounced slightly on the balls of his feet, and start a comfortable dribbling whose unvarying flow might continue for a minute or more; he would even chat over his shoulder to pass the time, as women converse under hairdryers. The man in Meard Street had not been the old, bladder-shot Josh, though. He had been the young Josh, fresh in town and up for it.

By 2 a.m. I was having trouble staying awake when, on an A-road to the north-east of Swindon, my eye was caught by a layby cafe called Babs Place. It was the usual mobile home affair, but it had a hygienic air about it and, most importantly, it appeared to be open so I pulled in. Plastic tables and chairs were arranged outside beneath parasols advertising a now defunct brand of lager. A large trellis partly covered the corrugated side of the cafe, and up it grew a variety of plants of different foliage and heights. The place had a kind of mad class, I decided, as I walked in. Inside, a fat woman was reading a fat book. She left it spine up on the table when she saw me, and squeezed herself behind the counter. She used only the best ingredients, she assured me, which was why her prices – she gestured at a board – were slightly more than you might expect to pay in a run-of-the-mill roadside establishment. She reached into the fridge and brought out a hamburger which she displayed gingerly in the palm of her pudgy hand as if it were a frog on the point of hopping off. 'See? Not an ounce of fat.'

I agreed to have the hamburger, with a side salad of avocado and pine kernels, and took my mug of tea to a table. I now saw that the woman – Babs, presumably – was not reading Danielle Steele or Catherine Cookson, as I had assumed when I saw the thickness of the book, but Clausewitz *On War*. On the walls hung framed Maxfield Parrish prints, of cerulean blue oceans and sun-soaked classical ruins. 'How far are you going?' asked Babs abruptly as she dabbed cooking oil from my burger with a square of kitchen towel.

A different sort of man would have shot back immediately

with something like: 'How far d'you fancy?' But I think too much, that's my problem. Instead I paused, stirred my tea, a picture of self-containment, while inside my head words spun furiously. When the dark brown tea was also nicely spinning I laid the spoon on the table with the merest click and said: 'Ipswich.' That was bad enough. But then, fatally, I elaborated. 'Well, not exactly Ipswich,' I went on. 'It's actually a few miles to the south-east, just where the rivers Orwell and —.' I had lost her, of course. And when I resumed my journey I cursed a lost opportunity, though the precise nature of that opportunity eluded me. I just knew that Josh would have known what to say, would have got Babs going.

I reached Ganges at daybreak. Only it wasn't HMS Ganges any more, despite what the road atlas said, but a police training college. Outside a sentry box, a policeman in white gloves stomped about to keep warm, his mouth blowing balloons of breath. The mast was still there though, rearing up through the dawn. I gazed up at it from the perimeter fence. I approached the sentry, who looked at me oddly before allowing me on to the parade ground so I could stand for a minute or two at the base of the mast. Down at the cottage, Josh had told me about this mast. The previous day Gordon had repeated these same stories and filled in some details I hadn't known. The mast had been a mythic thing but now here it was, made of wood and tension, its rigging singing in the wind off the old German Sea.

On most aspects of his time at Ganges Josh was reticent, but he loved to talk about the mast. The mast rose 143 feet from the centre of the parade ground and terrified the nozzers, who were told all sorts of lurid tales about boys being scraped, strawberry-jam-style, from the asphalt at its base. Part of the recruits' training was to climb it, the higher the better. The first platform, at the level of the mainsail, was known as the Devil's Elbow. This was reached by launching yourself out into thin air at an angle of forty-five degrees and hauling yourself up and over by means of ropes called futtock shrouds – the equivalent of an overhang in rock climbing. The platform above, in line with the topsail, was an elongated semi-circle known as the Half Moon. From the Half Moon, a Jacob's ladder led to within fifteen feet of the very top of the mast. For that final fifteen feet you had simply to embrace the mast and shin up as best you could. On the very top was a disc, a foot in diameter, known as the Button. For ceremonial parades, the most important being the annual Admiralty's Inspection, a boy was chosen to stand up here on top of the mast, to attention, with no means of support. He was known as the Button Boy. Every boy, in theory at least, wanted to be a Button Boy and in years to come many ex-Ganges boys would claim to have been Button Boys when they weren't.

Josh took to the mast immediately – later he would say he must have had a death wish – and was soon swinging around it like a chimpanzee in a tree. But none of the recruits, Josh included, had done the Button. The moment arrived one fine Saturday afternoon in the spring of 1948. By this stage the recruits were so familiar with the mast that they climbed it for fun, took their comic books and cigarettes up there and sat about on the Devil's Elbow or (the daring ones) the Half Moon, reading, smoking and chatting. Josh was on the Half Moon with a couple of others. After larking about for a few minutes they settled down to read about the Man with Two Brains and hardly noticed when Josh stepped on to the Jacob's ladder.

He didn't allow himself to pause when he reached the top of the ladder but embraced the mast as a randy dog locks on to a human leg and began to shuffle the final few feet upward. When he reached the top of the mast, he held on with one hand and with the other stretched up and grabbed the lightning conductor; paused, breathed deeply, and made his bid for the Button. There was a split second – when the metal lightning rod shifted in his hand, and his wild eye caught the rolling horizon of North Sea and Suffolk coastline – when he thought he was going to fall, become the strawberry jam of those stories told to scare the life out of the nozzers. But the conductor held firm, he felt the rushing of wind as he looped upward, and then his plimsolled feet were fighting for grip, his body was swaying into equilibrium, and he was standing on the Button!

The moment warranted a drumroll, but no one had noticed. Surely some sod would look up eventually? Looking about him, Josh must have felt something like a god. The sun burnt a vast slick of molten gold into the North Sea some two miles offshore. He looked down on the flying-boat station in Felixstowe docks, across the mouth of the Orwell. Those vast, winged pods, Sunderlands and Catalinas, were like pupae. He had to resist the temptation to lean over and pick one up. In the other direction, the spire of Harwich church was no bigger than an upturned drawing pin. If he dived he would fly, he felt sure of that ... 'Look at Avery,' came the shout he had been waiting for. 'He's on the Button!'

As a result of this feat Josh was chosen to be that year's Button Boy for the Admiralty's Inspection. For once he could look down on everyone, and even as important a bloke as an Admiral looked no bigger than an ant. Perhaps the respect Josh earned for doing the Button was enough to keep him reasonably happy at HMS Ganges. At any rate, he didn't bunk off but completed his time on that chilly littoral and then, after serving briefly on a ship called HMS Vanguard, received his first proper commission: two-and-a-half years at sea, thirty months away from England, aboard a frigate called HMS St Austell Bay.

On St Austell Bay, Ordinary Seaman Avery sailed the seven seas to the Far East and New Zealand, and, I suppose, worked a simultaneous passage from childhood to manhood. However, this time is another blank in his life. He mentioned it to me very little − losing his virginity to a prostitute in Piraeus in exchange for a packet of Player's, and having the woman's daughter the following night, being the most notable episode he recounted. He talked, too, of the *longueurs* of shipboard life, especially in the tropics; the way the body cooked lightly, day and night; the smell of hundreds of these slowly cooking bodies; the bunks buried deep in the fo'c's'le that were more like coffins than beds; the infestations and the murderous boredom. 'I even wrote some poems at the time,' he told me, 'so things must've been desperate.' Poems? I said. 'Oh they were just scribbles. I chucked them long ago.'

This wasn't true, however, for these poems turned up among Josh's meagre belongings after his death. They were scribbled in pencil on a sheet of furry paper headed MESS DECK ROSTER which he had taken from the ship. The sheet of paper had been folded and re-folded, until it was brown and shiny along the creases. The pencil script had been all but subsumed by the coarse and degenerating texture of the paper. Yet it was still legible, and that he kept these poems through the course of a peripatetic and largely possession-free life indicates they meant a lot more to him than he ever let on. They are not at all bad, either, given the age and circumstances at which he wrote them: short, simple, expressive of the monotony, physical discomfort and quiet desperation of life afloat in the tropics. We'll come to them.

Gordon said he didn't know much more than me about Josh's naval career. He just remembered Josh saying, when he returned from that long commission on St Austell Bay: 'I hate it. They treat you like shit.' But he was able to fill in some gaps. He showed me a group photograph from Ganges − a bank of boys as dense as a football crowd, with Josh's head ringed in Biro. I studied his face under a magnifying glass,

47

but can't say I recognized him. Gordon had also kept a felt pennant from HMS St Austell Bay, and another photograph, of Josh in bell bottoms sitting on a dockside bollard; 'Auckland 1950' was written on the back. It was in Auckland, apparently, that he had taken on a Maori in a brothel – Josh had been a useful boxer at Ganges – and broken his nose.

Gordon asked me if I remembered Josh's tattoos. What I remembered was that Josh had been ashamed of them. He always kept his right sleeve rolled down to cover up the one on his forearm – was it a heart, or a bluebird, a dagger or a serpent? I don't recall. The ones on his knuckles he couldn't cover up, but over the years the hairiness of his hands and the darkening of his ageing skin had pretty much done the job for him; so that where formerly there had been LOVE and HATE, a letter on each knuckle, by his late middle age there were just blue smudges. These tattoos, Gordon remembered Josh telling him, had been done in Singapore by a Gurkha known as Charlie Two Thumbs, who had had two thumbs on each hand.

Such details apart, the seas that Josh sailed will have to remain uncharted until he returns, after thirty sweaty, boring, crab-ridden months, to Devonport, where no one, among the welcoming crowds on the quayside, has come to welcome him. He has money and sexual energy to spend, and, after a brief, unhappy visit to Liskeard, he returns to Plymouth to spend both at a rate of knots. At some point in his knockabout progress from bar to whore and back again, showing off his tattoos, an idea takes root: he won't go back. He's still got nine years to serve, the best bloody years of his life, and he's buggered if he's going to serve them afloat. The weekend he's due back off shore-leave he cuts the labels out of his gear, ditches uniform, kitbag, mattress and hammock, everything except his greatcoat, in a rooming house in Plymouth and sets out for London. He has no money, he has no identity.

He is just twenty. Progress to London is slow. He walks, he hitches, he practises using different names, gets drunk. But all the time he is weaving closer to his home-from-home, his destiny.

Just why Josh landed in Soho, what impulse drove him there when he scarcely knew London at all beyond the mainline railway stations he had passed through (on his way to Devonport or Chatham, his khaki kitbag and his hammock, lashed up with seven half-hitches, slung across powerhouse shoulders) is anyone's guess. He himself had forgotten precisely how he ended up there, though he supposed he had known it by reputation; it was a favourite haunt of sailors, especially, during the war and after, even if that also made it a bit dangerous when you were on the run. It seemed to me, though, that Josh and Soho were simply made for each other, appropriately magnetized: all they had to do was stray into each other's forcefield to fall into an iron embrace.

So it was that he reached the edge of Soho one wet Sunday lunchtime in winter. He had a couple of bob, enough for a drink and he would take it from there. He walked into the nearest pub, dipped his hand in his pocket and was about to order a drink when a big, blond, soft-looking bloke sitting on the bar stool next to him chipped in: 'You're all wet! Let me buy you a drink. Please, it's on me.'

JOSH, MICHAEL LAW, NORMAN BOWLER AND HENRIETTA
MORAES, BY DANIEL FARSON (ESTATE OF DANIEL FARSON)

Chapter 3

An odd fish, Farson, terrible soak. Unreliable, self-pitying, cruel, bullying, yet strangely engaging. He built a career around Soho. He blathered and bored for most of his life about it, endless books, tedious recyclings of the same old stories. What on earth would he have done if he hadn't fetched up there as a young man, pink as new skin and on the make? Classically, Soho both made him and killed him.

In his autobiography, conveniently published after Josh's death, Farson pulls Josh to pieces, blaming him for his being fired from his job as a photojournalist on *Picture Post* and portraying Josh variously as ungrateful, feckless, exploitative and semi-educated. Here, for instance, is Farson describing a trip he and Josh made together to Italy:

> We continued to Venice where even the approach by train is spine-tingling as the skyline comes into view. 'Look,' I cried emotionally, 'Venice!' But Johnson was stuck in the corner with a comic book and did not look up. For the first time I felt a chill of dislike.

Jean was incensed by this poisonous little sketch, simply couldn't recognize the man she later knew. Certainly the reading matter I associate with Josh – spread out on the kitchen table of the Sussex cottage, jostling for space with the little bowl of salt crystals and the blue plastic pouch of Dutch rolling tobacco – is *The Times* (for the crossword) and the *Sporting Life*. But so what if he read comic books as a kid? Who didn't in the fifties and sixties? Jean reckoned Farson had chosen this detail of the comic book as an emblem of Josh's stupidity and Philistinism; anyone more interested in Spiderman than the Grand Canal had to be a hopeless case. It was pure spite. And it wasn't hard to work out where that spite probably came from: Farson never forgave Josh for not being queer.

His published account of his relationship with Josh makes good material for amateur psychoanalysis. Theirs was 'a strange romance'. Unlike your typical sailor, Josh does not like sex, shows no affection, remains unresponsive, and so on. On the other hand, he does enjoy getting drunk and beating several shades of shit out of Farson. Farson says these fights were routine, and describes them with surprising relish. They do it on old bombsites, where bricks and rubble are readily to hand as auxiliary weapons, and Farson always gets licked. He admits his skull is cratered with wounds, but he remains pretty cheerful about it. A saloon bar shrink might well say that Farson feels, deep down, that he deserves it, for being a filthy little queer; and that if being beaten up is the only point of physical contact with Josh that is likely to be on offer, he will take it.

The first night they spent together after meeting in Soho is breezily documented by Farson. He records merely that 'Johnson and I slept together that night in the single bed in my room because he had nowhere to go, but he seemed to have no interest in sex or affection, not like a sailor at all.' What he leaves un-said is rather more interesting.

At that time Farson was renting a room above a hairdresser's in Beauchamp Place. This chichi little street may be a toffs' ghetto now, lined with shops selling reproduction antique globes and hats fit only for Ascot, but in 1953 it was a repository of strangers wrapped in the loneliness of rented rooms, of human particles still settling down after the great dust-up of the war. There, after their session in the Mandrake, Josh returned with Farson and had a bath and shave, and Farson realized just what a beautifully feral creature he had netted. For Josh didn't have any belongings with him; no clothes bar the rags he stood up in, no personal effects, as if he somehow existed less than other people; more, in fact, like an animal than a human. The trousers of the old suit Farson 'lent' him (he never got it back) were much too wide. Josh bunched up a fistful of the waistband and still they were slack. 'Don't worry about that,' said Farson, and slung him a belt. 'Tie it tight and you'll look all the rage.'

They went drinking at the Bunch of Grapes, round the corner in the Brompton Road. They got drunk, of course, and at some point, back in the room in Beauchamp Place, Farson made a pass at Josh. Josh reacted badly: he punched him in the face, causing the black eye and swollen cheekbone that by the following day, when Farson took Josh to the Gargoyle for the first time, had coloured up so spectacularly. Josh recalled that he hadn't enjoyed hitting Farson; if Dan himself was a classic masochist, there is no suggestion that Josh derived sexual pleasure from inflicting pain. Josh wasn't a sadist but a pragmatist. If he was going to stick around with Farson it would be on the basis that, first of all, there would be no sex between them; secondly, that Dan would look after him, pay his way, make introductions, and in return he would give Farson what he craved: a bit of a hammering now and again. For all Farson's privilege, he lacked something that only Josh and types like him could give, and Josh knew this instinctively.

He also realized that Farson had something that he could give to Josh. It would have been easy, on that first night, to wait until the big blond man had fallen asleep and then slip away with Farson's clothes and a wedge from his wallet. A week before, *en route* from Plymouth, in some boarding house on the seamy side of swanky Winchester, that's what he would have done if the chance had arisen. But he was in London now and he saw gold glinting in the pavement. Josh didn't just want Farson's money, that was a short-term solution. He wanted something it was much more difficult to take. He wanted Farson's voice, the timbre of absolute confidence, of refinement and familiarity, that made him listened to and respected; he wanted the way Farson walked into a bar, so that people looked at him rather than through him. He was sick of subsistence survival, sick of being a scrote at the bottom of the pile. He wanted to be one of the officer class, who talked in ra-ra voices and just had to click their fingers to get what they wanted.

'I'm not really one of them either,' Farson had remonstrated. He pointed out that he was half-American, and had done his National Service in England as a GI in the US Army. He then told Josh a story from this time. Blond hair freshly razored to stubble by a German barber, new olive tunic chafing his fat neck, General Infantryman Farson had taken a train from Southampton to London in the company of a tweedy, top-drawer sort of English couple. His presence set them off. How superior to all Americans they supposed themselves to be! Swapping smug stories about the beastliness of Yanks, they treated Farson, the only other passenger in the compartment, as if he weren't there, or at least could not understand what they said. Indeed, with a raised eyebrow or a flicker of the eyes in the direction of the plump and clueless looking GI in the corner, they would enlist him as Exhibit A in much of their prejudicial drivel. As the train drew into Waterloo, Farson stood and touched the peak of his cap. 'S-o-o-o nice to have shared a compartment with you,' he drawled in his most patrician tones (so that 'shared' sounded like 'shard'). 'The insight it has afforded into your rebarbative little minds was most instructive. Good day.' And with that he smiled and was off, leaving the old couple gasping like fish.

'God I enjoyed that. The look on their faces! That's all you have to do to get on in this country,' Josh remembered Farson advising him. 'Talk proper. Act the part. And you can be anything. Even a pansy. You can be an outsider and they don't even know it.'

Josh was now ready for Soho, poised to enter the maelstrom. It was on the evening of the following day that Farson took him to the Gargoyle and introduced him to Francis Bacon.

Whatever happened to the Gargoyle? Needless to say, it is no more, its mirrors and dreams shattered long since. Is it any great surprise that, on the whole, I prefer to live in the past when you consider what they did to the Gargoyle in the name of progress? They gutted it. They collapsed the coffered ceiling, painted in gold leaf, and carted it off for firewood; they took the twenty thousand pieces of mirror, Henri Matisse's *effet éclatant* which characterized the Gargoyle experience, and put them in a hole in the ground in Essex; the red plush-and-gold chairs went to furnish rooms for rent in Bayswater; the glittering ballroom became an industrial space to let. The dreams and drunkenness lay among milk cartons and tabloid front pages.

The Gargoyle came to an end some time in the sixties. It was empty for a while – the aforementioned industrial space – and then served for some years as an alternative comedy venue, where I went once. I wished later that I had paid more attention to the surroundings, but how could I have known that this was where Josh met Francis, that this was where the ball started rolling? There would have been little left to see, but I had never needed much visual or atmospheric stimulus to set me off. And a spot of daydreaming would have helped distract me from the dreariness of the comedy act, which consisted, as far as I can remember, of gags about bidets and erections.

The second time I visited the place where the Gargoyle had been was after Josh had died, and this time I knew what I was looking for. The comedy club had closed and the floor the Gargoyle used to occupy had become the offices and studios of a small post-production film and TV company. It had a conference room with a long table, a couple of glassed-in booths and an editing suite. There was one other thing I managed to see before I was bundled out by a snooty and suspicious receptionist with rings in her eyebrows ('You look weird,' she said. 'I think you better go.' '*Me* weird?' I said). In one corner I noticed that a section of the false ceiling was hanging loose. When I peered behind it I saw fragments of the old moulded ceiling: swags of fruit, cascades of grapes. To think who else would have gazed on them, head back, in their cups ... It was an exciting moment.

I liked to visit Soho. I felt at home inside the square mile itself, this corner of an English field that will be forever foreign. The feeling I attributed earlier to Dan Farson, a surge of relief akin to that experienced when physically leaving the country on reaching Soho's streets, was actually my feeling, what I felt, though no doubt the half-American and wholly gay Farson felt something similar. My problem was the getting there, having to cross those vast tracts of Outer and Inner London that ring Soho like bubble-wrap round a velvet-lined box. Once I was there though, in the box, with the lid down, I felt invisible as I never did elsewhere. That's because Soho can be what you want it to be. And some people, believe it or not, wanted it to be Croydon. In the early seventies the entire area, from Regent Street to Charing Cross Road, from Oxford Street to Leicester Square, bad and beautiful Soho, of backstreet industry and below-stairs debauchery, came within a whisker of going the way of its most famous club. Westminster Council approved plans for 'comprehensive redevelopment', a grandiose scheme to turn the whole of Soho into a tundra of shopping precincts and car parks. Imagine, the streets that Blake and Shelley and De Quincey trod, flattened beneath double yellows and another Rumbelows. Well, it didn't happen in the end, but the will was there. This is what can happen in the present, which is why I tend to play it safe by staying in the past (though the past, too, can let you down, as I would learn).

And so I lived Soho's history when I walked its streets. A regular sighting of mine was Thomas De Quincey in perpetual, restless quest for Ann, the saddest story that Soho ever told. On any evening, at six, he can still be seen, near the bottom of Great Tichfield Street just before it flows into what he called the great Mediterranean of Oxford Street, his etiolated features, his sunken, haunted eyes, looking ghastly in the gaslight. He waits there because it is the agreed point of rendezvous with a fifteen-year-old prostitute who once saved his life and whose kindness he could never forget. The year was 1802; the man who later succumbed to a fiendish opium habit was eighteen years old and sharing a derelict, rat-infested house at thirty-eight Greek Street with an abandoned ten-year-old girl who believed its echoing rooms were haunted. Each night, he and this waif huddled together for warmth on the floor of one or other of the rooms, their heads resting on a bundle of old law papers, their only blanket a tatty coach-man's cloak; and in the day, while the little girl worked in service, De Quincey walked the streets to keep warm and occupied, often in the company of a prostitute called Ann.

Arm-in-arm, faint with hunger and cold, Thomas and Ann would take the air of Oxford Street and Soho, in unconscious parody of the nobs over in Mayfair. On one occasion De Quincey collapsed on the steps of a house in Soho Square.

Uttering a cry of terror, Ann ran off to Oxford Street and returned with a glass of port and spices. This potion revived him and he remained forever convinced that without it he would have died. A short time afterwards he had an idea to pay Ann back. He decided to visit a friend outside London to borrow some money, which he intended to share with her. He took the Bristol Mail from Piccadilly one dark winter evening. Ann walked with him as far as Golden Square where they sat down and said their farewells. Ann, so he writes, was overcome with grief and foreboding at his impending absence. She put her arms round his neck and wept into his collar, unable to speak. He reassured her that he was likely to be gone only a week at most, and that when he returned he would find her on her usual patch. But if for some reason he could not find her, or his business took longer than he anticipated, she should wait for him every night at the bottom of Great Tichfield Street at 6 p.m. until he showed up. And so, after urging her to get some medicine for her violent cough, he boarded the coach. But he had omitted one thing, and it was to prove crucial. He did not know her surname, and had not thought to ask her what it was.

Just three days later De Quincey returned to London, his business concluded much earlier than he had anticipated. But, even in that time, Ann had vanished. He hunted for her everywhere, hampered and frustrated by his ignorance of her surname and the understandable suspicions of the street people he questioned. He found the street but not the house where she had been lodging. He questioned her acquaintances. And every night he returned with a hopeful heart to the bottom of Great Tichfield Street. But she never turned up. De Quincey described Ann's disappearance, the mystery of her fate, as the heaviest affliction of his life. He tortured himself with the thought that through London's mighty labyrinths he might have passed within a few feet of her and not known. In

59

countless thousand female faces he sought in vain her singular sweetness of expression. And ever after he would be struck at odd moments, in solitary places, with grief and love for the girl who saved his life and whom he could not repay, and would find himself weeping.

Just another big city story, as De Quincey himself acknowledged, but it resonated particularly with me; for Josh was my Ann. I sought him, the truth of him and what he did, but I too was destined never to find him. I too was hunting high and low, rummaging in the bin bags of his life, buttonholing his friends. What is biography but failure, however glorious? Oddly enough, somebody else had already thought of the Ann parallel in respect of Josh – Dan bloody Farson, wouldn't you know it. A few weeks after they first met, Josh did a bunk, wearing a gaudy waistcoat Farson had bought him in the Burlington Arcade. Farson turned Soho upside down in pursuit of his new friend: 'I searched with all the desperation of De Quincey in pursuit of Ann,' he wrote.

The De Quincey story aside, though, it was mostly Soho's post-war era that materialized in my mind's eye. This is when the confluence of personality and ideas, the congruity of time and place, reached the ripeness of a Golden Age. It happened in Montparnasse in Paris in the twenties and Haight-Ashbury in San Francisco in the sixties. Our turn came in Soho, London, in the fifties. When I walked that matrix of Dean, Frith and Old Compton Streets, I scarcely saw the bars that looked like welding workshops and their black-clad denizens, I heard just the briefest snatch of their mockney accents and mobile-phone bleeps. I hardly noticed the blokes in macs hawking filthy vids along Brewer Street, the *Big Issue* sellers, the crack-addicted beggars with dogs on string, the bicepy gays in Old Compton Street windows and the half-famous television faces outside Dean Street's private drinking clubs, though (a sound bit of advice, this) I did always remember to keep half an eye skinned for motorcycle couriers since one of them almost had my left leg in Wardour Street.

In my Soho the shopfronts were small again, selling ukelele strings and sheet music, cummerbunds and shoe lasts. There were Italians on Brewer Street and black dudes in neat Caribbean suits on street corners. There was a sandwich-board man advertising matinées at the Palace Theatre, and cheroot smoke spiralling from an open window. There were smells that rotated me through the compass points of Europe and beyond – Polish cabbage and Russian tobacco, French bread and Italian sausage, Swiss cheese and Turkish coffee. Pencil-slim girls in headscarves and A-line skirts, with conical breasts, nodded as they passed by. Miraculously, while the rest of Britain, indeed the rest of Europe, nursed a monochrome post-war hangover, Soho had colour. It was not the kind of colour we have today, which is saturated, very often fluorescent and certainly exhausting. This was knocked back, dusty and dusky, the red of red wine, the green of vine leaves, the Technicolor of old movies. Can you see and smell what I'm getting at?

All this, though, is background. Now, lurching into the frame, comes a genuine Sohoite – Nina Hamnett, say. Nina has the requisites: a youthful beauty ravaged beyond all recognition, a talent cheerfully tipped down the toilet, one of those fluting upper-class voices ('My deah' here and 'Ducky' there) that post-war, egalitarian Britain is to find increasingly irksome and anachronistic, and a drink problem of improbable dimensions. Nina, once a model for some of the century's great artists and an accomplished painter in her own right, is in her sixties by 1953, and looks, well, hideous. What price now the paeans of praise from Sickert and Augustus John, Gaudier-Brzeska and Modigliani? She wears sticky dresses held together by their stains, she soaks the bar stools she slumps on with her pee. Her hair hangs in rat tails and her nose has the look of a root vegetable. In the French Pub and the Fitzroy Tavern, where she ekes out her remaining days, she has an old Oxo tin she rattles for contributions and a party trick which she threatens to perform if you do not pay up: she will show you her breasts, whose state of decrepitness is only to be guessed at. 'Modigliani said I had the best tits in Europe,' she will tell you, or in a reference to Gaudier-Brzeska's damaged sculpture, *Naked Torso*, 'I'm in the V & A with my left tit knocked orf.'

Listen to this account of her young childhood in Saltash in the 1890s, which Nina wrote in 1932. 'Next door lived a boy of about six. I spent much time trying to pull him through the wire netting which separated our gardens, but without success; he is now, I believe, a Brigadier-General in the Royal Engineers.' Then consider the manner of her death in December 1956: she fell forty feet from the window of her bedsitting room in Little Venice and impaled herself on railings. Verdict: accidental death, despite the discovery of a stool placed at the open window.

Was it really like that? It was, it was.

Another exciting moment was seeing for the first time the photograph of Josh in the French. I was given it by Jean. After Josh died Jean had sold Greensands and bought a classily converted barn in the Northamptonshire countryside with views from the first-floor sitting room of an Iron Age tumulus in a distant field. She had dug out various items for me relating to Josh's life, and his death, such as the pencil written poems from his St Austell Bay days and the envelope she received from the mortuary containing the few quid and the betting slip. I had already spotted the print of John Deakin's moody portrait of Josh, the right side of his face entirely in shadow, hanging on the wall of her staircase. Now she told me about how she'd been stoned when she first set eyes on Josh, how the room had been spinning and he had seemed like a very still centre of things. Then she produced the photo, or rather a smudged photocopy of the photo. It had been torn from a magazine (*Picture Post?*) and showed four people sitting round a bar table. It was captioned as follows:

The Soho effect: a sailor enjoying his shore-leave to the full [i.e. Josh], the film producer Michael Law, Norman Bowler, a bodybuilder, and the delightful Henrietta, otherwise known as Mrs Michael Law. Say cheese, Henrietta!

It had evidently been part of one of those fashion and lifestyle features that *Picture Post* and lesser periodicals went in for in the fifties. The location, as verified to me subsequently by both Law and Bowler, is the French pub in Dean Street (they recognized the square-topped, square-legged table. I checked the tables out for myself. They've been replaced with those standard-issue pub tables with wooden tops and decorative wrought-iron bases). I was grateful it was the French. Since the demise of the Gargoyle, no venue so embodied the spirit of fifties Soho as the crammed and smoky York Minster – known generally as the French since it entertained members of the French Resistance, including De Gaulle, during the Second World War. Its successive landlords, Victor and Gaston Berlemont, were the hub of a madly spinning wheel of post-war bohemians – Bacon, Freud, Farson and so on. Josh too. Though I had never doubted his stories, this photograph made them more real. I couldn't stop looking at it.

The four celebrants – of some long forgotten event, or merely perhaps of life, their enormous good luck in leading the lives they led – are laughing uproariously. Henrietta has her mouth open so wide you can see the delicate flying buttresses around the tonsils. Though they are drinking out of coffee cups they are pretty obviously plastered, so the picture was probably taken after hours when, so Josh told me, coffee and tea cups were provided into which you could tip your own alcoholic drinks. A clear glass sugar dispenser of unmistakable fifties design – squatly phallic – stands next to a large, square ashtray brimming with butts and bearing on its side the blurred, illegible name of a whisky or cigar brand. Josh and Law hold up their coffee cups between thumb and forefinger whilst, in identical poses, also holding aloft smouldering cigarettes. It is late and there is no tomorrow.

It was, as I said, inexpressibly satisfying and exciting to find my first image of Josh *in situ*, as it were, deep in the territory I had otherwise mapped out for him in my head. He sits in the left foreground nearest the camera wearing a tweedy, rather itchy looking suit. In the right foreground is the rounded back of an empty chair where one might assume the photographer to have been sitting prior to standing up and taking the picture. Probably it was Dan Farson, who would certainly have been sniffing around, and was still working for *Picture Post* as a photojournalist at the time. Whoever holds the camera, he must have said or done something to get a reaction at the moment the shutter clicked, hence, in particular, Henrietta's expression. Josh, nearest the lens, grins blithely, looking entirely at ease.

I can't say I'd have recognized him without the caption identifying him, erroneously, as 'a sailor enjoying his shore-leave to the full'. His head is more boxy than in the Deakin portrait, where there's something of the grinning ferret about him. Here his smile is boyish and guileless. You could see why people might want to help him. But the most surprising thing about the photograph is just how relaxed Josh looks. The picture can't have been taken that long after he first came to Soho. Yet here he is, a boy sailor from nowhere, mixing easily with Soho's bohemian élite. Michael Law, a documentary film

64

maker when the picture was taken, had served as a naval officer in the war; yet he rubs shoulders happily, and literally, with Ordinary Seaman Avery. Norman Bowler, who went on to find a fame of sorts as Sergeant Harry Hawkins in the television series *Softly Softly*, was then a bodybuilder (he worked out with Sean Connery when he was still called Tom Connery) and the friend of the troubled painter Johnny Minton, who committed suicide in the late 1950s. Henrietta was to pick up the torch of decadence that had been lit and carried with such flair and dedication by Nina Hamnett. She was married to both Michael Law and Norman Bowler and became known as Henrietta Moraes after her third husband, the Indian poet Dom Moraes. Famously, she was model and muse to both Lucian Freud and Bacon, whose painting *Lying Figure with Hypodermic Syringe*, featuring a naked Henrietta on a striped mattress with a needle in her arm, tells you all you need to know about the poetic degradation of her life.

And so I cherished this smudgy image for accidentally capturing a perfect moment, the moment whose spirit I wished to make sense of and celebrate in words: of Josh, of me, and you, and all of us, oblivious of our fates.

'Smile, for God's sake,' said Farson. He lifted his camera with the large flash mechanism jutting from the top and waved the group closer together. 'You look like a bloody undertakers' convention. This is supposed to be, you know, what a happy bloody part of town we carouse in, we gilded young things.'

'We're loaded,' said Norman Bowler, 'that's why. I've drunk enough to sink a battleship.'

'Float one,' said Henrietta.

'Nothing wrong with undertakers,' said Michael Law. 'I knew one once, had a greyhound. Raced it at White City. Called Memento Mori.'

Josh turned to Law, blinked as he tried to focus his red eyes. 'Could you see its ribs?'

'Eh?' said Law.

'Was it so thin you could see its ribs? The greyhound?'

'Aren't they all?' said Law.

'I hate that,' said Josh. 'Poor bloody sods. Starving them then making them run like the clappers. What sort of a life is that?'

'It's like bodybuilding,' said Bowler.

'Can you just shut up and concentrate,' said Farson.

'It's nothing like bloody bodybuilding, Norman you arse-hole,' shouted Henrietta. 'I was going to go home with you tonight but I've changed my mind. Too late. Sorry. I'm not going to bed with an arsehole.'

'Suit yourself,' said Farson.

'Come on now darling,' said Law. 'I think we're getting a wee bit silly.'

'Oh yes, that was very silly of me, to contemplate going to bed with Norman. Terribly sorry Norman. What I meant was, I'm going to bed with Mick.' She leant across the table and planted a slobbery and lingering kiss on Josh's lips. He didn't precisely respond, but neither did he pull his lips away. Law looked at the ceiling in exasperation.

'Sit down!' screeched Farson. 'Please. You're not sleeping with anyone, not yet anyway. Just one sensible minute from you is all I ask. This is supposed to be an article about how bloody fantastic Soho is, do you see? You've got to look merry, not half-dead. Full of wholesome *joie de vivre*.'

'I want to be full of something else,' said Henrietta, and then, pouting, to her husband, Law: 'Pardon my fucking French.'

'Is there any of that brandy left?' said Josh to Bowler. 'Stick it in there.' And he pushed his coffee cup across the table.

'One last try,' said Farson. 'Bunch in a bit and smile ... I said *smile*! I give up. Bloody hopeless.' He lowered his camera. 'Where's that brandy?'

'Aren't you supposed to make us laugh? Say cheese or something?' said Law.

'Yes go on Dan, give us laugh,' said Henrietta. 'Show us—.'

'For God's sake,' said Law. He shook two cigarettes from a packet, handed one to Josh and lit them.

'You could always tell us how you got your black eye,' said Bowler.

'That comes under the heading of private pleasure, and as such is off-limits,' said Farson. 'I know what, though. Try this one on. Mick, tell them what you said when you met Francis the other night in the Gargoyle.'

'Oh yes,' said Henrietta. 'Do tell, Mick. Do tell what you said to Francis the other night in the Gargoyle.'

I saw it all. I was standing at the bar and they were tucked round the corner on the left at the back. Needless to say, I couldn't believe it at first. I was up in town for my bi-annual meeting with the property editor of the newspaper I wrote for. Twice a year I would steel myself to visit the newspaper's Docklands offices and submit myself to a limp lunch of grilled chicken and frilly salad with a teetotaller with disconcerting, purple-tinted specs. In return I received the score commissions that would keep me busy and solvent for the next six months. It made me feel like a hermit coming down from the mountain to beg scraps from the mother monastery. On this occasion, he had seriously suggested I go to southern Spain and try to find an old East End villain or two so I could lampoon their ghastly villas in the hills. Sometimes I wondered if he was trying to get rid of me. As I often did, I retreated to Soho to lick my wounds, those psychic lacerations wrought by exposure to boring people and corporate architecture. It was shortly after Jean had given me the copy of the photograph and I decided to check out the furniture at the French to see if it matched the picture.

I was standing at the bar with a glass of Macon Villages, studying the photocopy of the picture which I had just unfolded from my Filofax, when I heard his voice. I heard Josh speaking! 'Was it so thin you could see its ribs?' he said. I know it is impossible, literally incredible, and I certainly wouldn't blame you for not believing me, but it's true. 'The greyhound?' he said. The voice was different, of course, from the one I had known. There was still a pronounced Cornish burr in it. It was the voice of a young man. But it was *his*; his pitch, his signature. And so I turned round, suddenly sweating all over, half joyous, half terrified. And there they were, in the corner, the five of them. Blond, bulky Farson was facing me head-on, but so engrossed in the mechanics of his camera that he didn't bother to look up and notice me. Josh was to one side and certainly couldn't see me. How thick and black his hair was! I had imagined it to be so, but the reality was even thicker, even blacker. The skin of his cheek and nose was slightly satiny with drink, but unlined. His teeth when he smiled, and he had a more or less permanent, drunken smile on his face, were pearly white. Can one's heart stop beating with shock? In the seconds that stretched to lifetimes that I took to drink Josh in, it seemed that it must be so.

Then I saw Henrietta. Her lustrous dark hair, highlighted by lamplight. The side-on swell and easily imagined weight of her right breast. The sexual energy that came off her like the shockwaves that follow an explosion. Francis Bacon never painted her direct. He worked from photographs taken by John Deakin. Deakin photographed her naked on her bed in all sorts of poses. More poses in fact than Bacon had asked for, including close-up beaver shots. Henrietta later caught Deakin selling prints of these pornographic shots to sailors in the French, a story that Farson dined off till he died. But it is not until you have seen Henrietta in her prime that you understand what she must have been like naked, on a bed. Did Josh sleep with her? He certainly wanted to, just as I did in those heartstopping moments that I gazed on her laughing, teasing figure in the shadowy corners of the French. She laughed louder than anyone when Josh repeated what he had said to Francis Bacon in the Gargoyle. Her mouth opened practically wide enough to admit the trunk of a giant redwood. If I'd been facing her I could have counted her tonsils. Her eyes blazed. She honked and snorted uncontrollably, to the point where she infected the others and they rolled about laughing, even Josh.

'Very good,' said Farson, clicking away, the flash going off with muffled detonations.

'You said that to Francis?' spluttered Henrietta when she had recovered her powers of speech. 'You're so sweet, Mick. I love you, I do.' She pinched Josh's cheek and pushed the end of his nose as if it were a buzzer.

Josh looked at Michael Law and got to his feet rather unsteadily. 'I have business to attend to,' he announced (Farson nodded and smiled approvingly at this), and lurched off to find the lavatory.

I couldn't help myself. I rushed up behind him and clapped him on the shoulder. When he turned round I yelled his name in a fury of joy: 'Josh!' No reaction. 'Josh! For God's sake!' But he just looked through me before dissolving into nothing. I stood there shaking, went back to the bar and ordered another glass. People were looking at me oddly. I couldn't work out what had happened. But then as I drank I calmed down and it became clear: he'd been called Mick then. Or Mike. Or Michael. Josh wouldn't have meant a thing to him. I had used the wrong bloody name, that was all!

DANIEL FARSON BY JOHN DEAKIN (CONDÉ NAST PL/VOGUE)

Chapter 4

Here's my chance to use one of those *Movietone News*-type scene-setters: In the Spring of 1953, as a nation still in the grip of rationing prepares to don its gladrags for the event of the century, the coronation of Queen Elizabeth the Second, Dan Farson and Josh Avery travel south, through a Europe slowly rebuilding itself from the rubble of war. Destination: the city of bridges and sighs. Hope you've packed your phrasebooks, chaps!

By the time of their Venice trip, according to Farson, Josh had managed to get Farson the sack from *Picture Post* (Dan's account of this event is garbled and implausible, while Josh had minimal recollection). Certainly Farson was desperately short of cash and finding it difficult to maintain the two of them at the required level of excess. Fearing, knowing, that Josh would disappear once his funds ran out, Farson had become reckless. His Rolleiflex camera – his means of work – was more or less permanently in hock in a pawnshop in Oxford Street. To a Bond Street dealer he sold off a bag of letters written to his great-uncle Bram Stoker, the author of *Dracula*, by Arthur Conan Doyle, Mark Twain and Ethel Barrymore. When he asked his father for loans, as he now frequently did, the famous foreign correspondent Negley Farson wondered whether his son was being blackmailed. And he was in a way: by his own, downward-hurtling infatuation.

Sometimes Josh felt like Farson's puppet; the next minute he would be Farson's master. One morning in Beauchamp Place, after Farson had insisted on combing and smoothing brilliantine into Josh's hair, he said to Farson: 'If I asked you to lie down and open your mouth while I pissed in it, would you do it?'

'If it made you happy,' Farson replied.

It was fortunate for Farson it was morning, that they hadn't had a drink. If Josh had been drunk he probably would have held Farson to this. As it was he merely replied, 'You're as mad as I am. Madder.' What he really thought was: *too* mad. Josh learnt a lot, though, from Farson. On their nighttime forays into Soho, funded by Farson's daytime pawning, selling and borrowing, he absorbed the literal and emotional topography of the place. He made sure, in the French or the Gargoyle, the Carlisle or the Caves de France, that he was noticed. He cultivated, in his lip and eyebrow language, an ambivalent sexuality that intrigued both men and women; caused them to make a mental note to return to this strange new boy and find out more. He fetched and carried drinks, offered around cigarettes bought with Farson's money, and wiped smudges of lipstick from the rims of ladies' glasses. He remained silent while conversation flowed around him; so still was he, so enigmatically unanimated his features, he seemed after a while like a rock around which pointless water flows.

This worked particularly well late into the evening, when everyone was drunk and befuddled. Then he could seem like the only worthwhile and solid thing amid the smoke and saliva. Beneath the shrubbery of chatter, people – Johnny Minton and Henrietta Law/Moraes, for instance – would sneak intrigued and lustful looks at him and he would nod or shrug, or, occasionally burst gloriously into that wide, shiny-white, irresistible smile. 'Painter Mick' or 'Mick the painter', he was known as, in honour of the blooper he had made when he first met Bacon and which in any case – a measure of how he was instantly liked – had been elevated to the status of a clever riposte.

With Farson at his side it was surprisingly easy for Josh to fit in. Like Josh, they were all acting anyway. Their stages were the bars and clubs. Where they all applied their grease-paint, and removed it afterwards, where they retreated to psyche themselves up for another gruelling session, was generally not known or cared about. They walked through those etched-glass doors and performed, just as did Josh. Covering up his past as he did the tattoos on his forearms, Josh claimed that he *was* a painter, a painter and decorator that is, working on the restoration of some of central London's bombed-out buildings. This wasn't quite good enough for Soho's drinkers and dreamers, though. In no time, prompted slyly by Farson who intimated Josh's immense modesty, they had talked him up into a real painter, of oils on canvas, who, like Lucian Freud, merely did the decorating stuff to earn money. Josh had been horrified by this. 'What if they ask to see my paintings?' he said to Farson.

'Oh they're not interested in paintings,' replied Farson. For now, he managed to persuade Josh that it was for the best. Being a painter, said Dan, daring to stroke the hair on the nape of Josh's neck, suited Josh very well. After all, wasn't he from the land of Velázquez and Picasso? Hadn't, somewhere, some of that blood-dark brilliance rubbed off? It was at moments like this that Josh let Farson know he had gone too far. All he had to do was lift his knuckles. And sometimes, when drunk and brimful of self-loathing, Farson would want to be hit; would goad Josh one effete put-down too far. Then Josh would whack him, with a perfunctory spurt of arm-and-fist that sent Farson sprawling in bruised glee. After an admittedly strange fashion their relationship had a balance and symmetry that kept it wobbling along for a while.

On this occasion Farson did not back down. He meant what he said about Josh passing himself off as a painter, he said. Had he been anointed a writer, Josh would have been expected to dazzle with conversational wit and insight; an actor, with flawless mimickry. But, notwithstanding the glorious freak that was Francis Bacon, a painter was little more than a watchful eye. Like Lucian, he could keep to the shadows and observe and be thought frightfully clever, which was where Farson's early advice about keeping your mouth shut came in. And Josh discovered that it worked. From Farson's point of view it was beginning to work too well. Josh was becoming known and liked and he was getting restless. Already he had made a couple of passes at women he had met in the French. Knowing his attachment to Farson they had not encouraged him, though no doubt they wished to. But one day he would disappear with a woman and not reappear. Meanwhile, the more he went without sex – he and Farson never had any kind of sexual contact after that initial mis-understanding – the more he drank and the darker grew his moods.

It was against this background that Farson bagged a double assignment out of *Picture Post*'s rival, a weekly called *Illustrated*. He was to travel first to Lake Como to cover the filming of an Ealing comedy called *The Love Lottery*, with David Niven and Peggy Cummins; then on to Venice, where the screen version of *Romeo and Juliet*, starring Laurence Harvey and Susan Shentall, with Flora Robson as the Nurse, was also in the middle of filming. Farson was delighted to have the work, but in a dilemma over Josh. He knew that if he left Josh behind he might never see him again. But taking Josh to Italy might be a nightmare, as it had proved on the *Picture Post* assignment which had resulted in Farson's dismissal. There was also a major practical problem: being on the run from the navy, Josh would need a false passport.

It was thinking about the ill-fated job for *Picture Post* that made Farson's mind up. He had been sent to a farm in the South Downs in Sussex – near the house that Jean would buy many years later and call Greensands – to write and photograph a story about a donkey of alleged rare intelligence. The donkey, so it was said, could count, but he wasn't merely an equine egghead: after a hard day on the calculus there was nothing he liked better than a pint of bitter. The story thus comprised four irresistible magazine elements: surprise, humour, sentimentality, and fur. Not to mention a fifth: complete bollocks. So Farson and Josh went down to Sussex, with Farson driving a borrowed car even though he did not have a driver's licence and had only the haziest grasp of how to drive. By the time they reached the farm, after several pub stops on the way, Josh was asleep on the back seat and the bonnet of the car contained an improbably deep and round dent such as might be made by the impact of a meteorite. The farmer, called Alwyn Hunter, turned out to be a drunk with a hip flask permanently glued to his lips. The donkey, with a coat as stained and fleabitten as a pub carpet, bared its baccy coloured teeth, swivelled a wild eye, and brayed, but could not be persuaded to add or subtract. Its apparent predilection for a pint at the local was a similar fiasco. Hunter said the beast had been banned from the pub 'on account of he shat absolutely everywhere'. The best that Hunter could do in terms of a photo opportunity was offer the donkey a swig from his hip flask. He grabbed the donkey by the ears and yanked his head back while Farson got his camera ready. At this point, with the farmer poised to plug the hip flask in the animal's mouth, Josh put in his appearance. Lurching towards them with a look of incredulity and horror on his bleary face, he yelled: 'Give it me. *Me!* Not the fucking donkey'. The animal's reaction was sudden and violent. The camera was dashed to the ground. Hunter, Farson and Josh retreated to the farmer's front parlour, to dress the farmer's bite wound and drown their sorrows. The story never appeared.

Farson reckoned that Farmer Hunter was an ideal person for Josh to impersonate when applying for a passport, as the real Hunter was not likely ever to get round to applying for one himself. Farson traced the farmer's birth certificate at Somerset House, and within a week Josh had a passport in the name of Alwyn Cyril Hunter – and another alias to add to his portfolio. Shortly after that, 'Alwyn Hunter' and Dan Farson departed from Victoria station for Italy. Farson was a widely travelled and cosmopolitan type, but for Josh the trip must have been a strange experience. Josh himself was widely travelled, of course, but only ever in an institutional way and always arriving from the outside, the open ocean. Now he was in the thick of things, in a train in dead of night, outside Nancy or Basle or Lucerne. Only fastidious men in hats of the softest felt travelled like this: border lights and throat-rasping coffee, and saturnine functionaries in kepis who say: *Votre passeport, Monsieur*. Did he love it or hate it? He did both, simultaneously, I was coming to realize. Just think of those knuckles.

There were signs, from the beginning, that Josh was working up to something on this trip. First stop was Lake Como, where Ealing Studios put them up in a room with two single beds in the Hotel Mira Lago in Bellagio, that exquisite resort of cobbles and oleanders balanced elegantly on the pudendum between the lake's two legs of water. When the waiter, in the restaurant that night, shook out Josh's linen napkin and glided it on to the knees of his itchy suit trousers, Josh glared at him as if the man had been sick in his ear.

'I've fixed up to see David Niven first thing in the morning,' said Farson breezily. 'He's got the use of a Bugatti, apparently. We might go for a drive up in the hills, take some lunch. I'm sure you could come along, if you like.'

'No thanks,' said Josh.

'It's not every day you meet David Niven.'

'I don't give a monkey's about David Niven.'

The Mira Lago faced the lake; their room was at the back, above the kitchens and courtyard. The next morning, from their bedroom window Josh gazed down directly on to a rack of half-roasted guinea fowl cooling in the yard. He opened the window, lit a cigarette, and tapped ash down on the semi-cooked birds. Farson had left to meet Niven without having breakfast. It was at these moments that Josh felt useless and destructive. Without Dan he dared not go down to the restaurant for breakfast. The man who had smashed a Maori's nose half-way across his face was afraid of a poncy Italian waiter with a ballet dancer's waist! But it was true. He gobbed on the guinea fowl for good measure, watching the elasticated skein of spit dropping slowly like a block-and-tackle on a winch. He would be expected to mooch about for a few hours on his own, then Farson would return to regale him with breathless tales of celebrity and he would grin and nod with gritted teeth. Then they would drink far too much and matters would, more likely than not, descend into a violence they could neither of them entirely recall the next morning, though the cuts and aches would tell an accurate enough story.

Still leaning on the window ledge, Josh rooted about in his trouser pocket and produced a grubby piece of paper. He unfolded it from eighths into a foolscap whole, revealing the paper to be of a flecked-grey, slightly furry type. From repeated folding and unfolding, the creases had acquired a brownish, shiny patina. At the top of the sheet were printed the words MESS DECK ROSTER; below, written in pencil in a small and deliberate hand, and scarcely decipherable in some places from fading, were columns of words that formed, when seen through half-closed eyes, blocks on the page that looked like windows in the façade of a large, many roomed house. Josh studied these columns of words intently. His lips moved, but produced no sound as he read and re-read the sheet of paper; he frowned; he cocked his head on one side. He folded the paper up, replaced it in his pocket ... then drew it out again, and considered it afresh.

Finally, with an abrupt show of resolve, Josh folded the paper back into his pocket, threw down his cigarette among the guinea fowl and went rummaging in Farson's suitcase. He was still wearing the itchy suit Farson had lent him on the first day they met. The cuffs of the jacket were sticky with dregs and there was a cigarette burn in one leg of the trousers which he had hacked at with a razor blade and thereby made much worse. Through this charred hole, when the light caught it, shone his right shin bone. He worked in a frenzy of dramatic anger through Farson's case, throwing unwanted items back over his head, until he found what he wanted: a brand new pair of khaki pants and a brand new shirt, both still in their brown paper wrapping. He tore off his sticky, smelly suit and tatty shirt and put on these fresh clothes. Josh was stocky and powerful, especially in his shoulders, but Farson was a much bigger man; though the shirt fitted Josh, the trousers looked comically oversized. Josh considered himself in the wardrobe mirror. He took the belt from his old suit and wore it as tight as he could, he rolled up the bottoms of the trousers. He pouted at himself, then went for a walk on the lakeside promenade, beneath the oleanders and limes, past the *belle époque* villas painted the colours of *gelato* – pistachio, nocciola, vaniglia – bent on seduction.

The actress Peggy Cummins was that rare, if not unique, breed: a woman who singularly failed to fall for his rough-diamond charms. Every woman I talked to about him, from virgin to sexagenarian, agreed that physically, he held a powerful magnetic attraction. I needed to know what the woman looked like who diverged from this consensus. Though the name Peggy Cummins rang a bell with me, it did not conjure a face. So on my next visit to Soho I visited an intriguingly quixotic little store called Flashbacks, which contains, in brown paper envelopes and old Agfa print boxes, an encyclopaedic collection of publicity shots and film stills of just about any movie actor you care to think of, the obscurer the better, in fact, as tends to be the way with these labours of obsessive love. A quick rummage produced stills of Peggy Cummins from a variety of mostly forgettable movies from the fifties and early sixties, including *In the Doghouse* and *Dentist in the Chair*. From these I gathered that Cummins had been a strawberry blonde bombshell; not the icy Hitchcock type but earthy, possessable. I was disappointed to find nothing from *The Love Lottery*, to see precisely how she would have looked when Josh met her, but happy to discover that four years later she had starred in one of the unsung classics of British cinema, *Hell Drivers*, featuring Stanley Baker and Patrick McGoohan (with Sean Connery in a bit part). The still I found showed Cummins in a black-sequinned evening dress, with diamante choker and earrings and a lovely rise of eyebrow pencil, cupping Baker's head by the jaw and ears and staring at him earnestly. The harsh downlighting gives Baker's pitted cheek the appearance of the moon through binoculars. The caption on the back, in wobbly blue typewriter type, read: 'Lucy (Peggy Cummins) explains to Tom (Stanley Baker) that she does not love Gino, and that now Gino knows this.'

Josh found Peggy Cummins on a bench facing the lake. He had been looking for dark-haired Italians, but was drawn by her fair hair. She wore it beneath a headscarf but its tresses still fell down her back, catching the pale spring light glinting off the water; over the headscarf, sunglasses. Farson records that she was polite but cold when Josh tried to work on her. He did not mention that the impossibly large trousers made

Josh look so ludicrous she had actually laughed at him. It is more than likely that her antipathy was not personal, that she was simply fed up to the back teeth, after seven weeks in Italy, of the ceaseless attentions and chat-up lines to which women, especially blonde foreign women, are subject from Latin men. But she certainly wasn't pleased when Josh sat down at the far end of the bench and, after an elaborate show of sighs and love-sick gazings at the choppy, blue-grey waters of Lake Como, made his move.

'Why don't you come back to my hotel room?' he suggested. 'My friend has gone out for the day.' The view from the room wasn't the best, he admitted, but they wouldn't notice that.

'A room without a view,' she said. 'How awfully tempting.'

'No, it's got a view,' he replied. 'Dead chickens. Small ones. But as I say, we won't notice that.'

A wind blew off the lake. Josh's trousers flapped around his ankles, the roll-ups unravelling. Peggy Cummins lifted her sunglasses and peered, frowning, at Josh's legs; then she shook her head, snorting in derision. 'Dead chickens?' she said eventually. 'Are you demented? Do you know who I am, sonny?' In a swift movement she slid along the bench and raised her arms to Josh's face. He thought she was going to strike him but she cupped his head in her hands, yanking down on the earlobes. 'See that lake?' she hissed at him.

Josh told me, in those conversations we had in the cottage, that contrary to his reputation he had never been very good at chatting up women. What he was good at was getting chatted up, a sort of passive-active technique that women generally manage better than men. The Peggy Cummins fiasco certainly confirms this. It also explains the chilliness between Josh and Farson as they set off for Venice the next morning. Peggy Cummins had related the bone-headed chat-up attempt to the film's press officer. When the two of them saw 'Alwyn' with Farson later that day, they realized the clown-trousered seducer *manqué* on the promenade was the companion of the correspondent from *Illustrated* magazine (and, needless to say, Farson would receive no more commissions from this publication, either).

Seeing Venice for the first time tends to detonate dangerously extravagant tropes among the more poetically minded. For me, for instance, Venice is the only old lady I have met whom I seriously wanted to ravish. Farson had been there before but he was anxious to re-live, through Josh, that initial, time-travelling exultation; the balustrades and architraves, the lopsidedness and colour washes, the lapping lagoon and caressing light, the bells that echo up through centuries. He wanted, as it were, to stick his hand up Josh's back, work his fingers into Josh's jaw and palate, and have him open-mouthed with wonder. But Josh would not give him that satisfaction. Josh kept his head in a Spiderman comic and knew he had won.

The row simmered on. They checked into the Hotel La Fenice et des Artistes, next to the opera house, and, by Farson's account, ate tagliatelli with fresh peas and butter beneath chandeliers in the hotel restaurant. Leaving Josh drinking in a bar near the hotel, Farson then went to the casino on the Lido and won thirty pounds on the roulette wheel. He gave enough to Josh to keep him in drink for several days, then set about his assignment to cover the filming of *Romeo and Juliet*. By this point he and Josh were hardly addressing a word to one another. Farson would return from a day on the set, or an evening drink with Laurence Harvey, to find Josh either already in bed and snoring drunkenly, or still out on the tiles. Either way, they had reached dangerously low levels of communication. And so the stand-off grew with the sulky, sultry imperative of stormy weather.

It happened to be on Coronation Day that, figuratively speaking, the skies opened and the storm raged. Flora Robson invited Farson and his friend ('with the nice curly hair') to a party at the British Consul in Venice to watch the enthronement of the Queen on television. Josh declined to go. He said he preferred to get drunk. So Farson went without him, with the actress and some other cast members. He recalled that the afternoon was dismal and damp, and that Flora Robson was so moved by the pageant unfolding on the flickering television screen that she put on sunglasses in a failed attempt to hide the tears of pride and wonder that rolled down her cheeks and clung to the sides of that famously tuberous nose.

When Josh returned to the Fenice hotel, the manager was waiting for him in a state of high agitation. In his office he explained to Farson that there had been a terrible accident, and Farson thought for a moment that he meant that Josh – 'Mr Hunter' – was dead. In fact Mr Hunter, having lost the key to the hotel room, had battered down the door with a fire bucket, and threatened a bellboy when he tried to intervene. This was not all. Before returning to the hotel, Mr Hunter had smashed up the little bar nearby which he had chosen as his home from home for the past few days. Naturally the police had been called. Mr Hunter was now in a prison cell, and would not be released until the damage to the bar and to the hotel had been paid for.

Farson spent the last of his casino winnings paying off the bar and hotel. He picked Josh up from the police station and they checked into a cheap *pensióne* near the Rialto Bridge that smelt of tomatoes and turpentine. They had still scarcely spoken. Trying to make light of it, Farson said: 'Well Mr Hunter, what *have* you done?'

'I'm not Mr Hunter,' replied Josh.

Farson shrugged. 'Just trying to be friendly. You've cost me a lot, you know. Not to mention money.'

'And I'm not a painter,' said Josh.

'No,' agreed Farson patiently. 'You're a farmer now. Farmer

Alwyn Hunter, from Sussex, remember? I hope that's what you told the coppers.'

'Forget that stuff. I'm not a painter. I could never be a painter. But I could be something else.'

'What?' said Dan, nonplussed.

'I could be a poet. I could write poetry.'

'What's brought this on?'

'Nothing's "brought it on". I just write poems sometimes, that's all, and now I'm telling you.'

Farson sighed a long sigh. 'This is what all this has been about, isn't it?'

'It's not *about* anything.' Josh was getting worked up again.

'Fine. You're a poet. D'you want a drink, Mr Poet?'

'You don't believe me, do you? Well here, listen to this.' He pulled the piece of paper from his pocket, walked over to the window, unfolded the paper to the light, and read the following lines, coughing hesitantly as he went:

No drink
Just stink
Eyes blink
Can't think

'There's more.' Farson nodded. Josh continued:

Sampan
'Lectric fan
Sweaty man
Sun tan

'I wrote them when we were in the tropics,' he said. 'I've got scores of them.'

Farson told Josh that his poems had a certain naive charm. It wasn't an easy effect to achieve, in fact some people spent a lifetime trying and never got there. They drank and Josh felt good; so good he briefly considered doing Dan the big favour and sleeping with him that night in their cramped rented room. But in subsequent days Farson did not mention the poems again and it became as if that evening in a small, sharp-smelling room near the Rialto Bridge had never happened; as if the poems had remained locked and lifeless among the folded paper, and Josh had not tossed them like birds into the sky of Farson's mind.

The following week they returned to London. Two days after their return, Josh gave Farson the slip. The day before, perhaps sensing Josh's growing restiveness, Farson had taken him to the Burlington Arcade and bought him a waistcoat, an intricate and meretricious piece of work, after Josh complained of the shitty clothes he had to wear. The motif on the waistcoat was a pair of peacocks, one on each side picked out in green silk-thread on a gold and red background. The pinstriped booby of an assistant invited 'sir' to admire himself in a full-length tilting mirror. A peacock of a man stared back at Josh, brilliant-eyed and proudly caparisoned. When the assistant tilted the mirror, the peacock flew upward as if into a tree. 'Look at you,' said Farson. 'A proper toff, Mr Avery sir.'

His waistcoat went down very well. On what was to be his last night with Farson they sat in the French at the back, occupying the same table as on that night when he had met Michael, Norman and Henrietta. Michael Law was missing on this occasion – 'filming,' said Henrietta with a grimace, 'at an aerodrome in Lincolnshire' – and she was sitting on Norman's lap when they arrived. 'My God, Mick,' she said, 'you look fantastic. How was Venice?' She motioned for him to remove his suit jacket. 'How's that for a decent bit of schmutter, Norman?' And then to Josh, under her breath. 'I wonder what you had to go through to get that. No, don't tell me.'

85

'It's all right,' said Josh. 'He's at the bar. I didn't have to go through anything. It's not like that. Dan doesn't expect things in return.'

'No?' said Henrietta. And then to Norman: 'Darling, catch Dan before he pays and get me another, would you?' When Norman had gone she said: 'You're naive, dear Mick, if you think that.'

'I know what I'm doing,' said Josh huffily.

'So what are you doing bunking up with a pansy?'

'I'm queer,' replied Josh with a leer. 'I'm a pansy myself. Can't you tell?'

'Hah!' she said, and reached out and held his prick through his suit trousers. 'I don't think so.'

Josh had his back to the rest of the bar. He froze, studied the glass covering the framed playbills on the wall to see if he could see the reflection of Norman or Farson coming back to the table. So far as he could see, the coast was clear. He pushed against Henrietta's fingers.

Henrietta let go. 'Norman's coming back,' she whispered. 'Get rid of the faggot, you don't need him. You need me. I need you. Got it? Thanks Norman, you're a sweetheart.'

They stayed for a couple of rounds, then Norman insisted that Henrietta accompany him to dinner. 'I want to stay here,' said Henrietta. 'I want wine for dinner.' But Norman had promised Michael. And then he would escort her home.

'We'll leave too,' said Farson. 'Let's go to the Gargoyle.' The two pairs parted on the pavement outside the French. Farson and Josh walked north, crossing Old Compton Street and continuing up Dean Street. When they reached Meard Street they found a line of people standing out on the cobbles waiting to get into the Gargoyle. Plumes of breath and smoke rose off them. 'Busy night,' remarked Farson.

They stood at the back of the line. Josh began to hop from leg to leg. 'Christ I need a piss,' he said. 'I don't think I can wait.' Farson nodded towards the nether gloom of Meard Street and Josh said he wouldn't be long. He walked twenty yards, found an unlit corner and pissed satisfyingly, watching his urine run in eager rivulets among the cobbles. Before he buttoned himself back up he weighed his stiffening prick in his hand, imagining Henrietta's touch. Perhaps it was this action – and the thoughts that went with it – that prompted him to do what he did next. He turned and looked right, at the queue of people for the Gargoyle. Farson was now about four from the end of the line, the back of his blond head obtruding from the crowd. Then he looked left, at the orange square of light and winking cobbles that marked the entrance to Wardour Street. He walked left, keeping to the shadows, and slipped into the swim of Wardour Street. He'd done it, he'd got rid of the faggot.

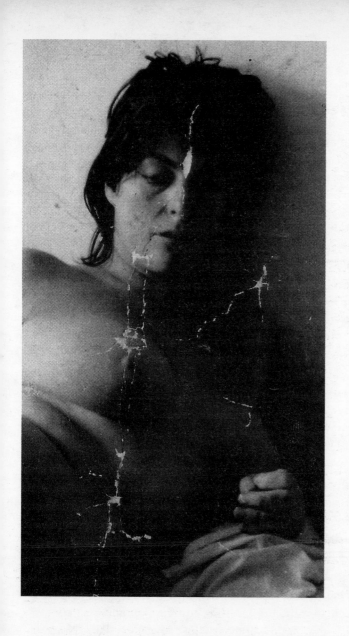

HENRIETTA MORAES BY JOHN DEAKIN

Chapter 5

His first thought was to find Henrietta. He gazed hopefully into a few restaurant windows before realizing this was pointless. He was surprised to find himself feeling suddenly vulnerable. He thought of the navy, the coffin-like bunk aboard HMS St Austell Bay, and even of the dormitory in the Derbyshire orphanage and the room back in Liskeard he had shared with Gordon and Swiz. These were places where, however miserable he had been, he felt safe, and the same had been true with Dan. He told himself everything would be all right, but momentarily he was feeling like a small child. It wasn't too late to return to the Gargoyle, spin a story to Farson about how he'd been suddenly indisposed. And this is what he nearly did. But then he caught sight of his reflection in a restaurant window. He looked good, capable of anything. Though he was virtually penniless, he also looked as if he had money in his pocket. He braced himself and grinned at his reflection. All he needed was a drink, and he would feel as good as he looked.

He'd been spoiled by his first weeks in Soho and his first encounter with Dan. He imagined that in this charmed realm it was enough simply to walk into a bar to be invited on a new adventure with a bunch of instant, buccaneering chums. In his astonishing waistcoat, how could he fail? Not yet knowing the neighbourhood beyond Dean Street, he wandered west from Wardour Street, dodging among the vegetable crates of Berwick Street market, and, after getting lost in a maze of ill-lit back alleys, ended up in a dingy dive in Beak Street. The bar was empty but for the barman, who was studying the form and drinking coffee or tea from a mug. Josh had just enough for a half of bitter. The barman pulled it without a word and returned to his paper. Josh took the drink to a table and drank it as slowly as he could, pretending to read the cards pinned to one wall: 'Let me Rebuild Your Physique (in private after 6 p.m.). For appointment phone GER 5346'; 'Visit Prof. "Cash" Cooper's TATTOOING STUDIOS at the Sports Garden, Coventry Street, Piccadilly Circus for Expert Tattooing'; 'Seeking that certain someone ...?' He told himself that someone – a woman – would walk in before he reached the bottom of the glass. After another drink, they would leave together. But he reached the froth and she hadn't appeared. He thought nostalgically of Farson's pick-up. 'You're all wet,' Farson had said. 'Let me buy you a drink.' He drained his glass noisily and left. The barman did not look up.

He spent that night in Golden Square. Evidently the bench he chose was the usual pitch of a tramp, for he was woken by a smelly, wild-haired man shaking his shoulder and shouting unintelligible imprecations. Josh hit him square in the face and the tramp staggered off. He lit his last cigarette, shivered and tugged the jacket of Farson's suit closed around his bright and boastful waistcoat; he missed his greatcoat. His only possession of note was back at Beauchamp Place and he doubted he would see it again. He gazed on the silhouettes of Golden Square's tall and narrow Flemish gables and thought of Henrietta. Was Norman poking her or protecting her? He didn't want to get on the wrong side of Norman, who was strong and fit. And how would he ever get to her without also running into Dan?

His immediate need was money. As soon as it was light he went to the underground lavatories in Broadwick Street and loitered there until a man – a dapper Italian – indicated they could do business. Did he absolutely hate having to do this, or did he accustom himself to it? I remember him shrugging, adjusting his seating on the tea chest, when I asked. It was just survival, and most people will do most things when that instinct kicks in. He turned another couple of tricks and by midday had enough money to keep him going for a couple of days. He went to the public baths in Marshall Street, had a bath and shave, ate bacon and eggs in a market traders' cafe in Berwick Street, then retraced his steps to Dean Street. He had worked out a way of dealing with Farson. The idea had come to him as he tossed off his second client of the morning and, for want of anything better to do, studied the obscene sketches on the wall of the lavatory cubicle. Among the usual horror-show of disembodied, oozing genitalia was a surprisingly accomplished version of Spiderman, with a huge phallus bursting from his spider suit. It made him think of comic books, the countless cartoon narratives he had been through at Ganges and aboard St Austell Bay. In one of them, an Indian brave joins the other side, the cowboys, and teaches them how to shake off pursuers the Indian way: the pursued doubles back to become the pursuer. By this simple expedient the Wild West is won. Rather than avoid Farson, Josh would seek him out, shadow him, keep him always in front.

So he took up position on the bombsite opposite the French and waited. Farson eventually arrived in the early evening. Josh watched him go in and remained across the street, waiting for Henrietta. But Henrietta did not appear, and after half an hour Farson emerged. Farson looked about him – for a moment, Josh thought he had been spotted – checked his watch, then headed up Dean Street. Josh followed, saw Farson into Meard Street and the entrance to the Gargoyle, then returned to the French. He knew Farson's habits. He would not go back to the French that night. Now Josh could drink there safely, and with a bit of luck Henrietta would show up. He ordered a bottle of hock with his hard-earned shillings and settled in for the evening.

I just missed Henrietta. I don't mean she'd popped out when I called to see her. I mean she died. The day after Henrietta's funeral – a gothically glamorous affair, according to the newspapers, featuring black-plumed horses pulling her coffin through Soho – I happened to be back in the French. It was midday, and I was standing in my now habitual place, propping up the bar towards the left-hand end, with one eye on the door and another line of vision into the alcove at the back, when an elderly woman walked in who seemed to be generally known. She nodded at some, grinned ruefully at others (acknowledging perhaps, some indiscretion of the night before) and said 'Darling!' to yet others while waiting for the barman to mix what was evidently her usual at this time of day, a bloody Mary. This woman was heavily made-up, her hair was dyed an improbable black, and a dewlap of flesh hung from her throat. Yet the ghost of great beauty still haunted her oval face. After insisting on the addition of yet more Lea & Perrins she drank deep of her pick-me-up, lit a Gauloise from one of those pale blue, crushable cartons and enquired casually of anyone who cared to listen, in the degenerate vowels of a patrician past, '*When* is Henwietta's funewal, again?'

I was about to chip in, but – another lost opportunity – a man in a toupee got there first. 'Too late, me dear,' he said. 'It was yesterday, didn't you know?'

'Ah well,' said the woman. 'What do I care? She was a cunt anyway. Fuck her.'

The woman (had Josh slept with her, too?), was right.

Henrietta, by all accounts, was a cunt. Soho was a cunt, come to that. One of the things that Josh kept emphasizing, down at the cottage, was that people got the wrong idea about those Soho days. They weren't like some rollicking film from which you emerged blinking in the late afternoon light, feeling glad to be alive. Yet this was the notion that people persistently took from all the accounts of the period. It wasn't their fault; the dishonesty of the chroniclers of that era misled them. The writers and journalists lied, said Josh. They left out chunks that they couldn't bear to face; the side of Soho that resembled a luxurious nightmare whose protagonists rushed ever more desperately through its dark alleys, impelled by the promise of – what? And when they got there, the final, blank wall at the end of the final rattrap of an alley ... Well, you may supply that chimera for yourselves. Henrietta was a spectre of one of these dreams. She was different, darker, than people imagined. She was a voluptuous goodtime girl who drank too much and had a laugh like a foghorn. Yes, she was those things. And she was a cunt, like dewlap-lady said.

Ah, but was it entirely her fault, her seemingly endless capacity for dishonesty, infidelity, drink, betrayal and the repeated, careless crushing of small dogs? It was the stuff about the dogs that fired me up more than anything, probably because it was a chance to get angry on Josh's behalf. One dog, so I was told on as good an authority as one is likely to find in the French on a weekday afternoon, went flying out of a fourth-floor window in pursuit of a pigeon after Henrietta had forgotten to close the window. This could happen to anyone. But shortly afterwards she reversed a car over its replacement, a dachshund like the first. This was not a coincidence but a pattern. Henrietta trailed a slipstream of damage and disaster. But can you blame her? What crises, to get back to the David Copperfield kind of crap, blighted little Henrietta's early life, and why did I care anyway?

I cared because I thought I was falling in love with her – not the real Henrietta Moraes, of course. No, I was falling for someone who looked remarkably like the Henrietta of the fifties. But what if Louise – that was her name – shared Henrietta's personality as well as looks? What if she was crazy and broke my heart? The physical similarity, based on paintings and photographs I had seen of Henrietta, was uncanny, so striking as to make it hard to imagine their minds being un-alike. Rather than condemn the real Henrietta, as plenty of others have done, I wished to understand her. I felt I needed to know what I might be up against. I first noticed Louise on the biannual visit I made to the newspaper offices for lunch with my editor. Not consciously, but I must have registered her, tidied her image away in some file in my head. That evening, when I was lying in bed back at the cottage replaying the extraordinary events of the day, I clicked on that file, watched it bloom into life and found myself staring at Henrietta/Louise. I had been going back over what had happened in the French, when I had been convinced, for those few moments, that I was hearing and seeing the youthful Josh. Of course it was nonsense, I acknowledged to myself in the black near-silence (just the odd call of a tawny owl) of the Sussex night: a combination of overwork, an over-fertile and feverish imagination and an increasing obsession with the details of Josh's life. I told myself I needed to chill out, maybe take a holiday. And then I saw Henrietta leaning over to press the button of Josh's nose; and, simultaneously, there was Louise, the swell of her breasts as she leaned to reach the fax machine, the way one pattern-stockinged leg lifted from the office carpet as she did so. The black hair and high cheekbones. The voice, languid and upper class, as she reminded my editor, the man in the purple-tinted specs, with an emphatic nod: 'Remember, you can't be too long at lunch. You've got a meeting at two fifteen.'

The woman who was a dead ringer for Henrietta, whose image I had just dredged up as I lay in bed, was my editor's secretary. I had had an electronic relationship with her for two years or more. Every week I would modem my article over to her with a curt note appended to the top: 'Louise, herewith copy. Any probs let me know.' But I had never set eyes on her till that day, had had no idea of her overwhelming, angry sexuality. My God! How I wished I had been more expansive, flirty even, when I had emailed and modemed her over the months. The die was cast now, though. There were parameters, etiquettes, concerned with electronic communication. Emailers establish their personality by the vocabulary they choose, their chattiness or brevity. To change suddenly would invite a suspicion of ulterior motives. Well, I decided, let her suspect! I would freely admit to having ulterior motives. And so, in the few weeks after the flesh-and-blood doppelganger that was Louise crashed into my life like a thunderbolt, I adjusted my electronic personality to make myself more attractive and intriguing to her.

I started off simply enough by adding a 'Dear' to soften the rather peremptory 'Louise' with which I had hitherto opened my communications. Then, on the second or third week after first setting eyes on her in the office, I mentioned casually that I had been glad to see her at last when I came into the office, for even though we had not actually spoken it had allowed me to match her name to the virtual person with whom I had been electronically communicating all these months. No response, of course, but then I didn't expect it; she scarcely ever sent me messages back except to tell me when an invoice payment had gone astray. Then I grew bolder. I mentioned, pretty casually, I thought, that she bore a striking resemblance to someone I knew (a bit of artistic licence there) who furthermore had been model and muse to the two greatest British painters of the century (i.e. Bacon and

Freud). Whenever Louise needed a mirror, I messaged her, she need look no further than the walls of Tate Modern or of the Museum of Modern Art in New York. I didn't use Henrietta's name, I simply dangled the bauble.

Nothing. No response. This time, I admit, I was disappointed. For two days, as I worked in desultory fashion on a dimwitted piece about how cutting-edge literati were all moving to North Oxford, I felt as low as I can remember. Then Louise emailed me. She informed me that the following week my copy would be required a day early as a bank holiday was coming up and they needed to get ahead 'production-wise'. Nothing else, no reference to the painterly muse. Yet my heart fluttered and lifted from the ashes in which it had lain. I discerned the hint of an encouraging smile through the ether, and it was enough to drive me on to reply with an email suggesting we meet in the French. I wasn't pushy about it. I merely informed her that I happened to be coming up to London at the end of the month and that my habit was to drop in at the French for a drink. As this was the same pub in which the woman who was a dead ringer for Louise (still I didn't use the name) misspent much of her youth, I felt it might be appropriate if Louise could find it in herself to join me.

What *folie d'amour*. In this moment, I lifted the trap door on my own private Soho.

Henrietta's father tried to strangle her mother while she was pregnant with Henrietta, who was born in Simla, India in 1931 and christened Audrey Wendy Abbott. When she was three, Henrietta was sent to board at a convent in Peckham Rye. She remembered looking out of the dormitory window one night and being terrified to see the sky looking red-hot and molten. It was the night the Crystal Palace burned down. In the course of a chaotic and peripatetic childhood, her alcoholic mother fell in with a rich woman who wore yellow waistcoats and ties and her hair in marcel-waves. They lived together in a rambling Northamptonshire mansion tended by a butler-and-cook team who were actually the exiled king of Latvia and his wife.

Henrietta married three times in fairly swift succession: in Rome to Michael Law, in Hampstead to Norman Bowler and in Chelsea to Dom Moraes, with whom she honeymooned in Greece in the company of exhibitionist American beat poet, Gregory Corso. While married to Law she had an affair with Lucian Freud. While married to Moraes, she attended the trial in Jerusalem of Adolf Eichmann, which her husband was covering for *The Times of India*. She said that the way Eichmann appeared in the courtroom – exhibited in a bullet-proof glass box – made him look like one of Francis Bacon's paintings of Pope Innocent X.

After giving up the marrying game, she fell in with upper-class hippy trash and lived a life of feckless, booze- and drug-ridden squalor in a variety of begged and borrowed houses in England, Wales and Ireland. The apotheosis of this degraded life was her arrest for breaking and entering – she gave the episode a romantic gloss by calling herself a 'cat burglar' – which resulted in her doing time in the hospital wing of Holloway Prison. Here she worked with other inmates packing plastic spatulas into tubs of cinema ice-cream. The women slipped the spatulas up their vaginas before putting them in the ice-cream tubs, which is why, she said, you shouldn't buy ice-cream at the pictures. Henrietta's children were mostly brought up away from her and did not feature prominently in her life. She was quite a gal. She was a cunt.

I imagined her growing old, losing the power that resided in beauty as she drank, pilled and mainlined herself into oblivion and premature decrepitude. A magazine photograph I saw of her in later years was all I needed to know of how she ended up, fucked by speed and Carlsberg Special. I keep in my mind how she used to be, in the black-and-whites Deakin took and Bacon transmogrified, of her naked on a rumpled bed.

As I say, I had been circling ever closer to Henrietta but she was to beat me in the end. My research into the Soho of Josh's era continued with the magazine cutting Jean had given me showing Josh with Michael Law, Norman Bowler and Henrietta ('Say cheese, Henrietta!'). Jean gave me Norman's phone number in Bristol. It was several years old but as far as she knew it was still working. Certainly Norman was still around, although in his early sixties, he appeared as the craggy love-interest in a telly soap. I called him and he told me that Michael Law was still alive, as was Henrietta, the mother of his two children. Everyone in that magazine picture, bar Josh himself, was still around and Norman was happy to put me in touch with the other two. For no particular reason I had decided to work left to right as they sat in the photo; in other words, I would see Norman first, followed by Michael Law, and finally Henrietta.

Norman lived in a Georgian terrace, what estate agents would describe as beautifully proportioned, distinctive, sought after and so on, on the side of a steep hill in Bristol. It was a foul day, a Sunday, when I drove there. Over Norman's shoulder, beyond the first-floor sash window, November rain fell in veils. This lofty vantage point, and the angle of the hill, created the illusion of an infinitely deep chasm beyond the base of the window, and as we talked I imagined those veils of rain flapping downward for ever. The tasteful drawing room – kilims, low-backed sofas in dark chenille, startling vases of cut flowers – was dominated by a full-length, practically life-sized portrait in oils: Bowler barefoot in white starched shirt, sitting on a wooden chair on a wooden floor, looking moody and chiselled in a male-model way. Johnny Minton painted it in 1953, he said. (The year Josh hit Soho. The Johnny Minton who was Norman's lover and who committed suicide.) 'There was a dark side to Soho,' said Norman in his faint west-country burr, repeating Josh's message. 'People don't remember those things now. People killed themselves. Relationships broke up.'

He spoke of Josh, of course. In fact he had provoking and unexpected things to say, things that would trouble me later. I don't wish to go into them now, we will come to them in good time. He was more lighthearted on the subject of Henrietta. When I showed him the magazine cutting – he had not seen it before, but immediately recognized it as having been taken in the French – he said: 'Henrietta with her mouth open, as usual.' He recalled a dinner party he had attended in London in the eighties. The broadcaster and writer, Robert Kee, had said to him: 'Norman, you were around in Soho in the fifties. Did you ever run into a woman called Henrietta Moraes?'

'Run into her?' replied Norman. 'I married her!'

'My God,' said Kee admiringly. 'You didn't!'

Henrietta had been impossible, he said: 'I would earn ten pounds and she would spend fifteen.' Norman dyed his hair and had had a hip replaced but was otherwise in amazing shape and could have passed for someone twenty years younger (he was sixty-six, the same age Josh would have been had he lived). 'I knew I had to get out of Soho or I wasn't going to survive,' he said.

Michael Law looked as if he hadn't left soon enough. He lived in part of a converted rectory sandwiched between grim London County Council tower blocks in the south London hinterlands, slap bang in the bubble-wrap that so unnerved me. The rectory looked as incongruous as a vicar in a darts team. Its parish had shrunk to a back yard, its door was daubed with a swastika that had survived attempts to scrub it away. Illness had made both speech and mobility difficult for

Michael. Like Norman, he was not familiar with the old magazine cutting I produced. He pondered it, remarked sadly: 'The scales fall from the eyes in old age. In those days everybody was thinking of what was in it for them – a time not so much of greed as of naked pleasure-seeking. There were a lot of loose cannons finding their way. There's never again been such a collection of people together in one place. Such free-range characters doing what they wanted to ...' He talked specifically of Josh, of course – as with Norman's comments, I'll address this later. The last time he ever saw Josh, he said, was at William and Hetta Empson's in Hampstead. Hetta had cooked a giant Mongolian dish. 'We had a pretty good supper and were boozing all night.'

He met Henrietta, his first wife, in the 100 Club, the jazz club in Oxford Street. 'We crossed Oxford Street to another world she didn't know about.' It was Michael who gave her the name Henrietta. 'Wendy wouldn't do at all. I named her Henrietta after my first girlfriend, Henrietta Swan.' Michael gave me Henrietta's telephone number in Chelsea.

The door swung open and Josh looked up for the fiftieth time, hoping to see Henrietta. But it was a small, furtive-looking man in an oversized Crombie. He had a swollen, drinker's nose and pockmarked cheeks and he looked about him with the air of one not used to buying his own drinks before he rummaged in his pocket for change. He spotted Josh. 'Oi, sailor boy,' he said. Josh didn't reply. 'You can't fool me, you know.' He nodded at Josh's knuckles. 'Want to see some dirty pictures? Pall Mall, the lot.' Josh shrugged and looked away. 'All right, fair enough. I can see you're the soulful type.' He sat down opposite Josh. 'Hang on a minute. I've seen you in here before. Aren't you the painter friend of Dan's? You on the run?'

'None of your fucking business.'

'Fair dos. It's just that I was in the navy myself once. I can see it a mile off. But I won't tell. Got a tab? Thanks. Now then. This'll cheer you up. Want to see the most beautiful and sexy woman in London. Naked. With her legs open?' He produced a large photographic print from beneath the voluminous coat and slid it across the table to Josh. Josh made to push it back, but then something caught his eye. He picked up the print and stared at it intently. It showed a dark-haired woman reclining naked on rumpled bedclothes with her legs apart. The shot had been taken from above her knees and showed her bush and labia. Her breasts fell amply to either side of the torso. Her head rested against the wall. She was smiling. Josh brought the print up to his eyes: it was, unmistakably, Henrietta.

'Steady on,' said Deakin. Josh replaced the print on the table. 'Ten bob,' said Deakin. 'Hours of innocent pleasure guaranteed.'

'Nah,' said Josh. 'Not interested.'

'Hang on,' said Deakin. 'That's a special rate for Her Majesty's armed forces. I'm pushing the boat out for you, Jack.'

'I told you: not interested,' replied Josh, puffing out his peacock chest. 'Why would I want to pay money for that when I can have the real thing for nothing? Oh, and it's not Jack, by the way. It's Mick. And it's not painter. It's poet. Got that?'

DEAKIN BY DEAKIN

Chapter 6

Like Josh, I found out all about the elusiveness of the woman you seek. Like Josh I spent long hours waiting in the French, and not a sign of her. I took a day off to do so, for Christ's sake. But Henrietta, the real Henrietta, sixty-odd, looking like shit and living in a Chelsea bedsit, had gone and died: had done the ultimate runner. Here was her telephone number in my notebook, as given me by Michael Law. Several times, after meeting Law and Norman Bowler, I had been on the point of calling her. Once, I even got as far as keying 0171 35— into the midriff of my cordless handset. But the speech I had prepared, the plan I proposed to put to Henrietta, was just too crazy for a first-ever conversation, and I chickened out. If she'd had email, now, things might have been different. You can take time to explain yourself, electronically. But you couldn't imagine her being online – by the end she could barely unscrew the top on that morning's bottle of vodka. Anyway, this was the idea that must now, thank God, remain forever unhatched: I would tell Henrietta that I knew someone who, from all the available photographic evidence I had seen, looked uncannily like Henrietta had looked in the early 1950s, before her looks and figure had been ravaged beyond recognition by all that unwise living. I would propose a meeting between Henrietta and this young and beautiful woman. It would be like stepping into a time-travelling mirror,

Henrietta Through the Looking Glass. Then, having secured Henrietta's intrigued assent to this meeting, I would put it as a *fait accompli* to Louise...

As for my cunningly casual invitation to Louise to drop into the French if she had the time, I had, of course, stressed that I would be in the French in the evening, as she would be working faraway to the east, in Canary Wharf, in daytime hours. But so obsessed was I at this time that I couldn't resist popping in early, 11 a.m. in fact, on the off-chance she had taken the day off and couldn't wait to see me. That was when I saw dewlap-lady. I had a glass of wine, and earwigged a conversation about Henrietta's criminal carelessness with dogs, but that still left practically a whole day to fill. I had lots to do – get money out from a cash machine so I could treat Louise to a decent bottle or two, pick up a photograph I'd ordered of Peggy Cummins from Flashbacks, buy a new ink cartridge for the printer, and mouse poison for the cottage (mouse urine was beginning to stink out the kitchen) – but I just had this unshakeable feeling that should I step out for even ten minutes, Louise would choose that time to pop her head round the door, see I wasn't there, and disappear from my life for ever.

I gave her until 2 p.m., then, already half cut, left the French to clear my head and do some errands. Trouble was, I couldn't stop myself doubling back to Dean Street every so often and peering at the doors of the French to see whether she might be going in or coming out at that moment. Once, standing in line for the cashpoint at the top of Greek Street, I convinced myself that she had just entered the French and was now looking round for me. As I stared at the hirsute nape of the man in front of me's neck, I shadowed her movements in my mind. She came in through the southernmost door. There was quite a lunchtime crowd and she stood at the edge ticking off the faces she could see before proceeding into the maelstrom. The man in front of me, whose head hair didn't finish on his neck but continued on below the line of his coat collar, had reached the cash dispenser. He was keying in his instructions – *beep; be-beep; beep; beep; beep*. Louise was craning her slim, nacreous neck to see into the alcove at the back of the French. I wasn't there of course, she would see that. With a reptilian sigh the dispenser dispensed a tab of paper with the balance of the man's account on it. He considered the piece of paper, screwed it up and put it in his coat pocket. Louise looked at her watch. It was possible that I was in the Gents; she would give me five minutes, then she really had to be getting back to Canary Wharf. The man hadn't finished with the cash dispenser. He issued further instructions: *beep; beep; beep; be-be beep*. Louise had given up on me, was walking out of the northern door. I left the queue for the cashpoint and sprinted down Greek Street; right into Bateman Street, left into Frith; right into Old Compton Street, left into Dean, swerving like a motorbike messenger. Madness, I know.

And so the day proceeded, and then the night. Off and on, between hastily run expeditions, I sat in the French for eleven livelong hours, watching those doors swing back and forth. In my pockets: bumper, 400-gram box of bromadiolone in handy-sized sachets; photograph of Peggy Cummins and Stanley Baker in *Hell Drivers*; wallet that grew less bulky as the day wore on; ink cartridge (the wrong sort, as it turned out). In my bladder at any one time: minimum one quart of white wine. In my heart: gaping hole, through which the wind blew ever colder ... I got to the point where it struck me as more likely that I would run into the twenty-year-old Josh than that Louise would show up. After all, however terrifyingly strange an illusion it had been, I had seen him in here once already, which was more than could be said of Louise. But I didn't see Josh either, despite my increasing despair and loneliness. And so, barely able to stand, I left the grinning mausoleum that the French had become at 11.11 p.m. (I know because I looked at the clock and was tempted to stay until 11.20, the full allocation of drinking-up time, on the infinitesimal fraction of a chance that she should still show up, before persuading myself that this was wishful folly and lurching off into the night).

Obviously I could not drive in this state. I could barely see. I staggered north-west, found myself eventually in a largish square: tall, thin façades against the red night, silhouetted trees as inky and eerie as in a René Magritte painting. Golden Square! Where De Quincey kissed Ann goodbye forever, where Josh made home of a bench. And here, also on a bench, I slept off the worst of the drink and, in occasional bouts of lucidity, dwelt on the nature of human perfidy. I wasn't just thinking of Louise, either. Josh, too, was beginning to let me down.

Have you ever, by sheer fluke, done something exquisitely well for the first time, and never been able to do it quite as well again? Write a love letter, make an omelette? Josh would never again enter the Gargoyle with quite the same head-turning insouciance he managed on that first occasion with Dan. Ignorance is a blessed thing. What, to him then, were Cyril Connolly and Hermione Baddeley, Jessica Mitford, Francis Bacon or Maynard Keynes? What price their poetry and mad ideas? He had walked among them, in that basement in the skies, and heads had turned. But now, now as he paced Meard Street as De Quincey before him had hovered in hope at the mouth of Great Titchfield Street, they looked through him. They hurried on their way to heaven, adjusting shawls and final-checking fly buttons, and did not notice the desperate scruff hankering to be invited in with them.

Abandoning Dan was proving trickier than he had imagined. He had thought he could just hand himself to

Henrietta, like a bonbon, and she would pocket him for consumption at her leisure, but Henrietta didn't seem to want to know. Perhaps she had decided he was a useless parasite. After all, she had no way of knowing that there were depths to him, that a heart beat beneath the peacock waistcoat, that poetry flowed from those fingertips that had burned themselves on stern lines and jacked off Italian waiters. But he could not get near her to reveal this fact. Why did Henrietta not come to him? He needed to get her on her own, then all would be well. She would invite him to her – what? Flat? House? Wherever she lived anyway. She would leave Michael Law, she would stop seeing Norman on the side, if indeed that was what was happening. They would be together. But he never could get her on her own. Dan would be there, or Michael, or a whole simpering flock of them, flapping noisily up Dean Street. When he saw them he would melt into the shadows. To be seen, to be caught out as a supplicant, would be humiliating. Besides, he was looking worse and worse. Dan Farson, he had to admit, had made him look a million dollars, with his brilliantine and cufflinks. Now Josh's lovely hair was coarse as rope; he'd pawned the cufflinks and the suit Farson had 'lent' him was sticky with the booze of too many bar tops and fraying at the cuffs; the waistcoat was now grubby and sad as a rotting peach. Some mornings he was so badly hungover he could not summon the energy to go down to Marshall Street baths, or, if he did manage to get there, achieve the focal length required to shave. The moral degradation of wristing off Bellini-eyed waiters for beer money in the Broadwick Street lavs was beginning to seep into his soul. If he showed himself to these gilded funsters bound for the Gargoyle he risked being taken for a human scarecrow, upon which to festoon their streamers of ridicule.

He did, once, manage to attract her attention. She was in the usual crowd – Michael Law, Dan, Norman, and two weirdos in kilts – and, as he hovered in the shadows of a Meard Street doorway, they caught him unawares by approaching from the other end, the Wardour Street end. The laughing, smoking group walked so close he could have cupped Henrietta's amber earrings in the palm of his hand. He held his breath, willing Henrietta to glance to her right. They walked past and he thought the moment had gone. But as they reached the entrance to the Gargoyle, Henrietta did indeed look round and back. His eyes locked on to hers. He widened them, beseeching her. She hesitated, then said, 'I've dropped something. I'll join you.' As they passed through the entrance arch, she ran back across Meard Street to where Josh stood. 'You've been following me, haven't you? Fuck *off*,' she hissed in his face.

'I need you,' he said.

'*I need you*,' she mimicked. 'Look, are you mad? You don't need me, I'm the last person you need. We need the opposite of each other, don't you see? Now kindly fuck off darling, for God's sake.' She skipped back across the street and disappeared into the Gargoyle.

Josh reeled. But he didn't let it put him off for long. She was, after all, in the gravitational pull of Michael and the rest. On her own, if he could get her truly alone, she would be different. And so he kept up his vigils. It was the ferrety little snapper, John Deakin, who finally gave Josh a helping hand, which is ironic because Deakin never knowingly helped anyone. Josh had reached the point where he was even considering handing himself in at West End Central as a naval deserter when he was recognized by the man who had tried to flog him dirty photographs of Henrietta in the French. Deakin, having calculated that the Gargoyle would contain at least half a dozen people prepared to fund his night's drinking, was hurrying up Dean Street when Josh asked him for a light. 'A light or a wank?' replied Deakin affably. Josh waved the half-cigarette he had rescued from the pavement and sighed. As Josh's features flared in the matchlight, Deakin said, 'Oh, it's you. Have you nailed her yet, sailor boy?'

Josh grabbed Deakin by the shoulders of his filthy mac. 'You know her? You know Henrietta?'

'Of course I know her. You can't shove a lens up someone's Pall Mall without being at least mildly acquainted.'

'I need to talk to her alone. Can you arrange it?'

'I can arrange most things if it's worth my while. What's the deal?'

'Whatever you like.'

'Come on, keep moving Jack, I'm dying of thirst out here.'

They walked as far as the entrance to the Gargoyle. 'Wait here,' said Deakin. He went inside. Josh pressed back into the shadows as a party of revellers arrived. He was on the point of thinking the pornographer had stitched him up when Deakin reappeared. 'This is the best I can do for you,' he said. He handed Josh a piece of paper. 'I've written an address on the back. Be there nine o'clock Monday morning and we'll sort you.' He scampered back up the steps and was gone.

Deakin had written: '103 Shaftsby Av. (side door).' Josh turned the piece of paper over. On the other side was printed:

APPLICATION FORM FOR
MEMBERSHIP
OF THE GARGOYLE CLUB

'To the Secretary, The Gargoyle Club, 69 Dean Street, W.1,' it continued. 'Please submit my name for membership. I agree to be bound by the rules and regulations of the Club.' There followed a number of categories to be filled in: Surname (BLOCK LETTERS), Christian name, Signature, Address, Occupation, Proposer, Seconder. Josh read it through twice. He realized that there was not a single category he could complete. He watched more people arriving at the club. He threw the application form in a puddle. He felt lighter than air, incapable even of pissing himself.

He was at the side door of 103 Shaftesbury Avenue at eight thirty on the Monday morning.

So what would you have Josh do now? I don't know about you, but I want him to take matters in hand, lead the narrative rather than follow it. I can't have him sleeping on that park bench for very much longer; he needs new clothes, before the current lot fall off him, and his hair, now stiff and matted, needs restoring to its former lustre. Oh, and I need him to get his leg over. Things are getting desperate in that department.

He's certainly not behaving as I expected him to, which leads me to the possibility that he was not quite the person I thought he was, or at least was not quite the person I wanted him to be. It was Norman Bowler who first set an alarm bell ringing. 'He was a sad man,' he said of Josh when I talked to him in his house in Bristol. 'All the people around him were producing – painting, writing, acting – and it must have been frustrating for him that he wasn't.' After Norman quit Soho, in the mid fifties, he and Josh fell out of touch. They were reunited in the late seventies in Brighton. Norman was appearing in a play at the Theatre Royal. Josh saw a poster for the play in Henfield, the nearest small town to Greensands, where he went twice a week to place bets. He had Jean drive him down to Brighton. They saw the play and afterwards Josh went to the stage door and passed word that he would like to see Mr Bowler. 'Tell him it's Mick Avery,' he said.

Norman said he didn't recognize him because he'd lost his hair – that thick, black hair – on top, and the years of heroic boozing had taken their toll. 'Mick? My God.'

'They call me Josh now,' he replied.

Norman recalled that practically the first thing Josh said to him was: 'I could have been you. I could have acted, I was as good-looking as you. What went wrong?' (And maybe, for all those years, Norman had been thinking, *I could have been Sean Connery.*)

'You didn't get out of Soho,' Norman said.

As for my thing with Louise, my madness continued. As I persisted in thinking of her as Henrietta, I fully expected her not to do me right. Have you ever slept rough, on a park bench, with a hangover, to be woken by unmitigated daylight? My condition that morning was just about the worst I have ever felt. After eating a bacon and brown sauce bap in an Italian sandwich bar in Wardour St, I retrieved the car and beat a zippy retreat back to the cottage, where I spent the rest of the day in bed feeling abjectly sorry for myself. It wasn't just the hangover, though that was bad enough. It was the rejection by Louise, who hadn't even had the good grace to let me know she couldn't make the meeting in the French. My initial impulse was to be proud and simply ignore her, give her a dose of her own neglect. But the more I thought about it, the more my distress gave way to anger and I knew that, at the very least, I needed to let her know just what I thought of her high-handedness.

The side door to number 103 was ten yards into a narrow cobbled street. The door itself, covered in peeling black paint, gave nothing away; no bell, no notice. In front of it, Josh hopped nervously from one foot to the other. He watched snouty delivery vans and horse-and-carts passing along Shaftesbury Avenue. Still twenty minutes to the appointment. He supposed that Deakin wanted him to appear in photographs. He assumed, having seen the print of a naked Henrietta, he would have to take off his clothes. He had made an effort to smarten up. His hair was still damp from the scrubbing he had given it with a sliver of soap he had found stuck to the tiled floor of the bath house in Marshall Street, and he had taken care to scrub himself extra clean, in case he did have to appear naked. He had shaved himself so closely he had taken the top off a spot half way between his chin and lower lip. Now it stung; he dabbed it gingerly with a piece of toilet paper. He felt ready. So long as Deakin could help him, with money and an introduction to Henrietta, he didn't mind.

Presently a woman turned off Shaftesbury Avenue and clattered up the middle of the narrow street in high heels. She wore a fur coat that brushed the cobbles as she swayed; her hair, tousled up into a casual bun, was black as mascara; her lips the red of deep-red roses. Her footsteps slowed as she neared Josh and the door to number 103. Having stared at her as she walked towards him, he now looked away, gauging her movement and position from the faltering sound of her heels on the cobbles. She had stopped less than a couple of feet from him! He felt his neck tense as he imagined her studying him. He felt ashamed of his stinking suit. He heard the rustle and tap of a handbag being rummaged in. He heard the repeated click of a lighter. He heard the luxuriating and sibilant exhalation of smoke. He smelt dark French tobacco. 'Cigarette?' He was so taken aback by the sound of her voice, he could only reply with a grunt. 'Would you like a cigarette?' she repeated.

He turned to face her. She held out a light blue packet. That voice! It was braying and degenerately elided. 'Would you', sounded like 'Ud yaw', and she pronounced her rs as ws. But, far from being chilly, as such accents generally are, the timbre had a warmth and frankness that made Josh want to disappear inside it. I assume that by now his own accent and manner of speaking had embarked on its journey from bumpkin to toff, and no doubt it was speeded on its way by the time he spent with Cecilia Winifred de Becket Graye. 'Kind of you.' He took a cigarette from the proffered packet and stared into her eyes. They were big and brown and unblinking. She held those deep red lips slightly apart between puffs on her cigarette, revealing a smudge of red on one of her otherwise blue-white front teeth. Her hair was a match for his in its casual lustre. He loved the way an errant strand fell in a curl across one eye; the way, with her free hand, she batted it away every so often. They stood stamping, smoking and smiling at each other in the cold morning.

'He's always late.' She nodded at the door, and Josh raised his eyebrows.

'Oh, like clockwork,' he agreed.

'You know what I'd really like? A bloody Mary.' She rolled her eyes. 'Just to get me functioning in all the right places. I hate it when he shouts at me when I'm feeling fragile.' Josh wondered suddenly if she, too, would be required to take off her clothes; if they might be required to do things together. The thought affronted him.

'Are you famous?' she asked doubtfully.

That she had asked the question at all made his heart beat faster. That she could think he might be famous! Beneath the peacocks, his thumping heart swelled.

'Well, not *famous*, I wouldn't say...'

'Or are you "unknown sitter"? That's what he calls people he just likes the look of. We had a tramp in last week. Peed in the corner. Place stank to high heaven. Of course Muggins has to clear it up.' Josh had the image of a naked, incontinent tramp, a scrawny, besmirched Christ, in a state of sexual excitement. What was going on? He suddenly fancied his suit was giving off waves of sourness and grease. 'Now let me see,' she continued, inhaling smoke and narrowing her eyes, 'which are you?'

'I'm neither,' he said. 'I'm just a poet. No one's heard of me ...' He waved an arm, dismissing a shortsighted, Philistine world.

John Deakin arrived at half past nine. The metallic crescents on his heels rasped on the cobbles. He hawked extravagantly as he neared them. 'Christ,' was all he said. And then, in between curses as he struggled with the key in the lock, 'You've met.' They nodded. 'Christ,' he said again when, having opened the door, he flicked the light switch on the staircase and the bulb blew. 'Lightbulb at lunchtime,' he said, to which Cecilia nodded. 'Got milk?' She nodded again. Fumbling in the gloom, he led the way up the narrow linoleum-covered stairs. At the top, on a small landing, he stopped abruptly and Josh ran into the back of his legs. Cecilia giggled. 'For Christ sake. Got a match, Jack? Be useful and strike a light.'

John Deakin made plenty of enemies. He was as unreliable as Henrietta – he managed to get sacked twice from *Vogue* – he cadged shamelessly, insulted people for fun, had the personal hygiene of a down-and-out, and liked shocking with his gratuitous crudeness. Barbara Hutton, the Woolworth heiress, described him, rather ingeniously, as the second-nastiest little man she had met in forty years after their paths crossed in Tangiers (he insulted her soft furnishings). George Melly remarked of Deakin that 'it's surprising he didn't choke on his own venom.' Farson called him 'the funniest man I had known.' He was a skinflint, a drunk and a scrounger, never known to have bought a round. He was a pockmarked little fucker who took fabulous, pitiless photographs. While Cecil Beaton and Norman Parkinson were fannying about with artifice, Deakin was dealing in truth, albeit the largely unpalatable variety. But, however many enemies he made, none hated him as implacably as he hated himself. This, at least, is our saloon-bar shrink's explanation for Deakin's attitude towards his own work, the best of which he did in the studio just off Shaftesbury Avenue.

I think of the ideal sort of studio as being the analogue of the creative mind; that is, simultaneously turbulent and calm, chaotic and ordered. My own modest 'office' in the cottage came nowhere near this. It is true that the slick hi-techery of the digital, slim-screen, green-light age, the power-point arrangements that look like space docking stations, were more analogous to the 'mind' of a robot. But even so, I do not by nature have the Einstein-haired bent to be both disorganized and productive. Hence my office was a dully ordered place, with a tin wastepaper basket (bearing the reproduction of a Stone Age gazelle-like beast found in a Dordogne cave painting) which I emptied every day, usually of discarded estate agents' specs of Home Counties stockbroker piles.

In the studio of the genius, so I like to think, the floor is a-swim with refuse and sweepings, with scrunched up paper, cigarette packs and broken cans. There is spattered paint and ink, snapped guitar strings and freelance piano keys; white dust and cobwebs and desiccated teabags the colour of fudge. But there is, too, the painting on the easel, its paint still wet and glistening; the resonating after-sound of a melody; the satisfaction of flowing prose well captured. From the foul rag-and-bone shop come masterful images. Well, Deakin's studio is certainly a foul rag-and-bone shop, but where are the masterful images? They are there, all right. In the forty-eight hours prior to Josh's visit, Deakin, in between sessions in the French and at least one prolonged bout of vomiting and fainting induced by drinking Parazone bleach in mistake for white wine, has photographed Elizabeth Smart, author of *By*

Grand Central Station I Sat Down and Wept, her husband the poet George Barker, Lucian Freud, Francis Bacon, and a bloke in specs from the BBC. These portraits are pegged on a washing line strung up across the studio. They are pristine at present, but soon they will join the other prints crammed into drawers and slipped behind cabinets, dog-eared, spattered with booze and bleach and God knows what, many of them to be lost to the world for ever. The negatives fare little better. They are binned, mislabelled, trodden on and cut up. If Deakin hated his own work so, can hatred of himself have been far behind?

Often, the incidental effect on the prints of such mistreatment is a happy one. That is to say that the tears and creases lend to the sitters an appropriately wrecked and desperate air. Take Peter Lacy, for instance, the superficially debonair former Battle of Britain pilot who was also Francis Bacon's murderously violent lover – he became a cocktail-bar piano player and died of drink. In a surviving Deakin portrait, his lips and the bridge of his nose are flayed back to white paper. A tear reaches from the edge of the picture to his jugular. Paint and inky thumb prints smudge his country-check shirt and Brylcreemed hair. His eyes are sunken, the lines beneath them thick and deep. The print is a palimpsest of pain.

But Josh was still young, the day he walked into Deakin's studio. And if he had had his share of pain already, he hadn't been stripped and whipped by it; it is good to see that the portrait Deakin shot of him that day was never damaged, for it is only right that he can still be seen unspoilt, in those days, those dog-days, when he still had hope.

Josh struck a match and Deakin plunged his key into the lock. He pushed and swore. The door was stuck. Coughing and spluttering, his eyes watering, he put his shoulder to it. The three of them popped like corks from darkness into light. Josh shielded his eyes from the brightness that fell from the ceiling lights in a blinding, immobile cataract. Deakin was bending down to retrieve from beneath the door the obstacles that had prevented it from opening. He picked up a flattened eggbox and a folded and torn contact sheet showing a man sitting and reclining in a series of poses on a bed. Deakin paused, regarding the contact sheet. 'Lucian's an old fox,' he said.

'*Deeply* attractive,' said Cecilia over her shoulder, putting down the pint of milk on a draining board in the corner.

'Never gives anything away,' said Deakin. He flung the contact sheet back on the floor. 'Christ,' he said. 'Can you do the honours with the skylights? My eyes are burning up.'

Cecilia took a stepladder and moved it into the middle of the room. She scooped up an armful of black sheeting and climbed the ladder. 'Steady the ladder would you Jack?' said Deakin. He filled a tin kettle from a tap. 'Just light the gas first, would you?'

Josh lit the gas and steadied the ladder. Before Cecilia had taped up the black sheeting against the skylights, turning the studio into a gaslit dungeon, Josh took a good look around him. His feet were planted in a sediment of torn photographs, news and magazine paper, cardboard, bottles and cigarette ends. On one wall, covering it almost entirely, hung a huge sheet of black velvet which was in fact several sheets stitched together by Cecilia. Arc lights on stalks hung down like tall men with sloping shoulders. Several large cases covered in tatty black cloth lay around. There were camera bodies and plate slides on the trestle table next to the sink and gas ring. Across the studio, like bunting across a street, hung photographic portraits pegged on washing lines. These, variously, showed a woman in a veil and a necklace of coins, a man in a flat cap, a man smoking a cigarette in front of a crumbling London terrace, a man that Josh recognized as the Francis Bacon he had met his first time in the Gargoyle, and a man in thick-rimmed specs with the emblem of a gentlemen's club or old boys' society on his tie. All the portraits were large and full face. No one smiled, all looked in some way guilty. Josh felt perplexed. There were no nudes. He couldn't imagine what he had been brought here for.

As Cecilia progressed with rigging the black sheeting over the skylights, so darkness fell in segments across the studio until it was illuminated solely by the blue flickers of gaslight beneath the tin kettle. 'Don't turn on the light yet,' requested Cecilia. 'I like this bit. Let's all have a ciggie first.' She slithered down the stepladder. Josh caught and smothered her in his arms, just for a second, but it was enough to make his heart race. She handed out cigarettes.

'Boil, you fucker,' growled Deakin at the kettle. 'Jack wants Henrietta,' said Deakin. 'That's why he's here. Isn't that right, Jack?'

'It's Mick,' said Josh. 'I just need to talk to her. Get her to see me on her own.' But already, his knuckles still humming from the brush of Cecilia's fur coat, he was wondering if this were true any more.

'Oh no, not Henrietta.' Cecilia sighed. '*Why* is it ...?' She left the question hanging, sighed again. 'Why don't men realize she's a cunt?'

Josh was shocked by the word. It defiled Cecilia's beautiful lips. Anger and disgust swept over him. What was he doing here anyway? 'Let's get on with it,' he said. 'Whatever it is you want me to do.' He strode to the door and flicked on the light switch.

'Relax,' said Deakin. 'Tea, for Christ's sake.' He jerked his head at Cecilia. And then to Josh, 'You don't have to do anything. Just stand there and look angry. Like you are now'll be fine.'

But by the time Deakin came to take the photograph, or rather the session of photographs, of which the print owned by Jean is the sole remaining evidence; by the time he had set up his tripod and found a stool for Josh to perch on, and Cecilia had lit, and placed in Deakin's sphincterish mouth a succession of cigarettes, which stuck there on his lower lip and he smoked without removing, sucking on them in quick rasps; by the time he had told Josh to discard the stool, pretend it was a Friday night, not a Monday morning, and to stand as if eyeing a tasty girl across a crowded room ('Pretend you've got the horn for Cecilia,' he said, and Cecilia was good enough to blush) and he'd got Cecilia to ruffle Josh's hair back and smear some Vaseline on it to give it some sheen; by the time he'd complained about the red spot on Josh's chin, then changed his mind about this too, and decided it looked so fine he would deliberately light that side of his face and have the other in shadow, and Cecilia had waggled the head of one of the lights-on-a-stalk until the soft, horizontal cone of light fell just so between photographer and sitter; and he had told Josh the story of the pornographic prints he had taken of Henrietta, pretending they were for Francis, and Cecilia had told Josh that it didn't matter if he couldn't fill out the form for the Gargoyle, she was a member and she would be honoured to take him there as her guest, and stuff Henrietta, who was, remember, a cunt anyway, but if he really *was* interested in her, that was the place to meet her; by the time Deakin finally bent to the viewfinder of his Rolleiflex, Josh was not frowning but smiling.

JOSH'S BIG BREAK: ADVERTISING PLAYER'S CIGARETTES WITH
VIRGINIA SLATER, PHOTOGRAPHED BY JOHN DEAKIN
(CONDÉ NAST PL/VOGUE)

Chapter 7

Not frowning but smiling. I like that. I've seen a lot of Deakin portraits and the subjects never smile. Not even Francis. Even Francis Bacon looks a bit bloody scared of Deakin's lens. Not that it was a cruel lens, according to Deakin anyway. He said he didn't victimize his sitters, he just exposed in them what they were usually too clever to reveal: the terror and melancholy and so on. What did he see in Josh, that cold Monday morning in 1953? Youth and happiness, suddenly uncomplicated by doubt; the desire to sleep with the woman in the fur coat leaning on the far wall of the studio who says, 'Coming to the French? I need that bloody Mary now or I'll die'; the growing conviction that he *will* sleep with her, before the week is out, or even the day. The happiest portrait Deakin ever took.

I too now knew happiness, such as I could not recall having felt for a long time. Louise had been in touch! I didn't expect to hear from her again, not after the email I'd sent her. It was, shall we say, strongly worded. Afterwards I wished I had allowed myself a cooling-off period before messaging her about her failure to meet me in the French, her blithe disregard of my kind invitation. In the past when I have reacted rashly in a not dissimilar vein, I have managed to retrieve the situation. In a fit of screaming frustration I once fired off a letter to the Karen that Josh had so outraged outlining the physiological cruelty of her position (or, as I pointed out – wittily, I thought – her refusal to take up a certain position) and the existential despair to which it was reducing me. Nothing wrong with that, you might say, but I had then veered off into obscene love poetry and foully intemperate, scatological insults which should really play no part in civilized discourse, even teenager to teenager.

After posting the letter, I spent all night in the school dormitory drowning in wave after wave of nightmarish denouements: Karen reads the letter and kills herself; she opens the letter at the breakfast table and bursts into tears, her father grabs the letter from her, reads it and decides to kill me; and so on. In the morning I awoke with a brilliant idea. When I had posted the letter the night before, the last collection had already gone. My letter still sat, like a ticking time bomb, in the red pillar-box just beyond the perimeter fence. Skipping breakfast, I hung about in the bushes near the pillarbox until the postman arrived in his van. I asked if I might have the letter back as I had changed my mind about sending it. He said I must be joking; to tamper with Her Majesty's mail was a serious offence which could land him in the slammer. When I offered him money – no more than 50p, I shouldn't think – he hesitated before nipping into the bushes with me and suggesting a different kind of payment. To paraphrase Josh, you worked the posties sometimes, you had no option, and the result is that I remained on such good terms with Karen that I became one of the favoured recipients of her Christmas round robin (she has a son and daughter – high achievers in, respectively, rugger and media studies – which at least goes to show that she did eventually abandon her principled stand upon attaining connubial bliss).

Email, of course, allows of no such retrieval. On this occasion I regretted sending the email to Louise a split second after pressing the 'send' button. I was hungover and self-pitying at the time. I shouldn't, for instance, have called her a 'heartless bitch', or indeed a 'brainless harpy'. The bit about 'types like her' needing 'hosing down' with the 'watercannon of reality' managed to be simultaneously pretentious, meaningless and sinisterly unpleasant. I sent the email on the evening of the day I had returned from sleeping on the bench in Golden Square. In mitigation, my body as well as my soul ached. And in a nightmarish rerun of that fretful night in the dormitory, I twitched and sighed all through the long dark hours, listening to the owls calling in the woods and imagining all sorts of outcomes.

There was no respite in the morning, no electronic come-back. I spent the day working on a piece about noisy neigh-bours. I'd interviewed a couple who lived below a deaf man with a history of mental problems who played his hi-fi at floor-juddering levels eighteen hours a day, but I couldn't do it justice. To be honest, I could have done with a noisy neighbour myself that day, something to distract me from thinking about Louise and the email I had sent her. The silence was accusatory. But I needn't have worried. On the morning after that, I had my reply. To her credit, Louise seemed to have taken everything in her stride. Her email wasn't effusive, but then again she wasn't that type. It said simply: 'We need to meet. How about—.' And she proceeded to name a pub and a time and date. But the best bit, the bit that really got me going, was at the end. 'You'll like the pub,' she had written. 'It's in *Our Mutual Friend*.'

Josh now embarked on a period of great happiness. Just as I did.

Cecilia was inspecting Josh's tattoos. She and Josh were lying in a large bed in her parents' house on a steep road bordering an edge of Hampstead Heath. Beyond the Georgian window, the leafy branches of a tree swayed against a morning sky of racing clouds. She kissed the bluebird on his forearm. She kissed the LOVE on his right hand, brushing her lips against the knuckles. 'I won't kiss the other one, though,' she said. 'It's horrid. HATE is horrid.' Now, her hair tickling his chest, she moved her lips towards his other forearm. 'What does that say, underneath the heart?' she asked.

'Mother,' he replied.

'Mother? That's nice. Where is your mother? You never mention her.'

'She's dead,' he said.

'I'm sorry,' she said.

'It was a long time ago,' he said.

'Do you remember her? What was she like?'

Josh laughed. 'She was the most beautiful woman in Liskeard. That's what they said.'

'Where's that? Is that where you come from?'

'Oh, nowhere. Where do you think?'

'God, I don't know. I'm hopeless. Manchester? Yorkshire? Tewkesbury?'

'Well it doesn't matter 'cos I'm here now.'

'So you are,' she said, 'and so am I.' He tried to pull her down beneath the bed covers, but she resisted. 'And you're a poet?' she said doubtfully, wrinkling her nose.

Being now almost perfectly content, he had practically forgotten that he was in the process of passing himself off as a poet. But Cecilia was a trusting and incurious soul, who would show no interest in actually reading any of his oeuvre. Besides, in Cecilia's world people had no need of lying; if Josh said he was a poet then that was what he was, and that was all there was to it. 'Of course,' he replied.

Looking relieved, she said, 'Good, I like you being a poet. "Mick the poet".' She lifted her hand to the window and wrote the words there. 'You'll know George Barker then,' she added.

'Barker?' He shook his head.

'You must know *George*,' she said. 'He's a poet. Matter of fact, Deakin was taking pictures of him yesterday. Wears a little peaked cap. Goes in the French. And the Gargoyle. Looks – poetic, I suppose.'

'I probably know him by sight,' said Josh. 'We don't all stick together, you know, us poets.'

'David Archer? – he's terribly nice. Awfully sweet. I always want to cuddle him somehow.'

'Maybe,' said Josh.

'He's Deakin's – *you* know.' She raised her eyebrows.

'I didn't know,' said Josh.

'Oh yes,' said Cecilia. 'Didn't you know? Couldn't you tell? Anyway, George is awfully sweet. God knows what he's doing with that runt Deakin. He runs a bookshop, even if he does look like a bank manager. I must introduce you.'

'Perhaps,' said Josh. He took her gently by the shoulders and attempted once more to tug her beneath the sheets.

'No I will,' she said, holding her head back for air. 'Show him your poems and he'll make you famous. He made George famous. *I* want to be a famous photographer,' she went on. 'That's why I'm working for Mister Horrid. *Vogue* have said they'll find me someone nicer to work with soon. He likes you, though, Deakin. I can tell. He doesn't just photograph anyone, you know. He's got plans for you.'

'What sort of plans?'

'To advertise something. That's where the money is, as he keeps saying. He'll have you wearing Silvikrin on your lovely hair' – she stroked it – 'or driving a super sort of car.'

'I don't drive,' said Josh. 'Besides, I told you, I'm a poet.'

'Prove it,' she said.

'All right, I will,' he said. 'Come here.'

'Do you still want to see Henrietta?' she said. 'I don't mind if you do, honestly.'

'Fuck Henrietta,' he said. He held her by the nape of the neck.

'No, fuck Cecilia,' said Cecilia. 'Fuck *me*.'

Afterwards Cecilia rang a bell and the household servant, Mrs Dollimore, who had white hair and wore a matching white pinny and bonnet, redoubtably and impassively brought tea on a tray and Cecilia and Josh smoked French cigarettes and dropped the butts in a half-empty glass of white wine left over from the night before. This was Josh's introduction to the world of feather beds and feather dusters, pinnies, deference, judicious bribery, and sugar tongs; of unhurried, uninhibited, amusing and powerful sex; of sex in the morning, watching, over Cecilia's shoulder, the swaying trees shaking their thrilling leaves, and sex in the evening, when Cecilia returned from work, against the sound of steadily falling rain. Cecilia's parents were absent from their London *pied à terre* not just for the day, or even the week, but for the *season* – gambling in Biarritz and Monte Carlo – a period that Josh could only think of in terms of time away at sea. Thus, in The Hon Edward and Lady Maud de Becket Graye's Hampstead town-house, he fulfilled his commission to screw their daughter and plunder their larder and cellar as spring warmed into summer.

They spent their days rattling happily around the high ceilinged, dado-railed rooms, waited upon by Mrs Dollimore, whom Cecilia was careful to keep clever, or across the road on Hampstead Heath, where, he recalled, Cecilia once knelt in the grass with the sun behind her shining through the translucent rims of her lovely ears, and her floaty purple dress spread like a fruit stain across the wild flowers. Since his naval desertion, Josh had always harboured at the back of his mind the fear of being picked up by the police and frogmarched off to Pompey and naval prison. At Cecilia's he felt, for the first time, entirely free of this fear. He dreamed frequently of being on his delivery bike and cycling through Cornish mornings with his happy dogs in tow. But now when he woke up it was not with a sickening jolt, the ghastly realization that life would never again be as simple and good. For life, he reckoned, was just about as good as it could get.

They caught the bus into Soho a few times in the evenings, and spent Cecilia's parents' money in the Gargoyle or the French, the Caves de France, the Pillars of Hercules or the Colony Room. Josh developed a generalized fear on these occasions, of being embarrassed or ridiculed. Why and by whom he hardly knew, but he was glad that they didn't run into Dan or Henrietta, Deakin, or the characters Cecilia had told him about, Barker and Archer. Once or twice Cecilia met an old typing-pool or deportment-class acquaintance and then Josh, mindful of Dan's advice, would remain monosyllabic and Cecilia's friend, overcome by his dark good looks, would swoon behind his back and prod Cecilia in stagey gestures of sexual envy. Josh grew increasingly anxious that one evening they would be faced with someone he didn't want to see and there would be a scene. At some point he would be ready for this, but for now he wished to enjoy Cecilia while it lasted. Claiming laziness, he persuaded her to remain in Hampstead in the evenings; they drank in the Flask or the Rosslyn Arms, or occasionally polished off a few bottles of vin de table, bought from under the counter of a *charcuterie* in Pond Street, while watching the moon rise over Parliament Hill.

Cecilia didn't want to miss out on Soho altogether, though, and so they reached a compromise. Josh would catch the bus down in the late morning and meet Cecilia on her lunch break. He managed to steer her away from the French and into the Gargoyle or the Caves for these lunchtime sessions. One reason for this was that Dan and Henrietta preferred the French. He had so far avoided any direct confrontations with them, though he had seen them once or twice across crowded bars. The French also admitted daylight. Daylight picked out the blackheads on Deakin's nose and the rime on his tongue. It streamed through those Dean Street windows and walloped the crapulent, the guilty and the suicidal in the side of their self-pitying heads. It made you drink faster than ever, drowning last night's hangover in the first curlings of a monstrous, yet bigger wave. Oh yes, lunchtime drinking in the French was an edgy, neurotic business.

The Gargoyle and the Caves, on the other hand, shared a lack of daylight, allowed you to take your time and route to reach a modicum of equanimity and equilibrium, before the whole crazy drinking pattern started to repeat itself. Like being barred in to the gondola of a ferris wheel, lunchtime drinking was the edging upward of the cabin as more people were loaded aboard below you. Josh much preferred the gondolas in the Gargoyle, which were upholstered and discreet. In the French, disputes were always likely to break out among the occupants of different cabins, and this was not wise when you were suspended so far above the fairground. Josh, especially, wished to avoid it. To flog the analogy, the optimum feeling was when you reached the top and, feeling like a king – feeling, in fact, like Josh standing on the Button – surveyed the whole world spread out before you. You held it as long as you could, but eventually you started to slip downward, and once that started, nothing would stop you.

Josh would pick Cecilia up from the studio at midday and they would go to the Gargoyle to drown their hangovers. Sometimes Deakin would come, too, though he generally preferred the French. Deakin had quite taken to Josh, which makes Josh one of the only two people to whom the jockey-sized shithead was reasonably civil (the other being Francis). He persisted in calling Josh Jack. He was pleased, he told him, with the portrait he had shot of him (another first – he generally expressed distaste for his own work). He brought in a rough print to show Josh, and Josh was puzzled and disappointed. 'It's all shadow,' he said. 'You can hardly recognize me.'

'Precisely,' said Deakin.

Deakin kept promising he would make Josh famous. 'I'll make you the face of the fifties,' he would say and, on the quiet, Josh began to feel his future might lie in modelling rather than poetry.

Sometimes Cecilia would be in the middle of a job when Josh called for her, and he would go on to the Gargoyle alone. The doorman, having come to recognize him, would nod him through on the understanding that Cecilia would turn up presently. On these occasions he would find himself drinking with what Cecilia, in the argot of the wild and nocturnal *habitués* of the Gargoyle, referred to as 'Dentists from Bird's Custard Land', suburban, 'professional' people who liked to frequent the Soho drinking club because it added a sprinkle of big-city illicitness to their lives. These people, who were perhaps Min. of Ag. penpushers from Sanderstead or tin-opener salesmen from Hillingdon, loosened their ties and slouched on the bar stools like movie toughs, but they were always back out of the door by two o'clock, and never appeared in the evenings, when the Gargoyle's true, louche denizens emerged blinking from their coal holes.

Josh had nothing against the 'Dentists'. His life had scarcely touched such people, and certainly no dentist, in the Gargoyle or indeed the mouth doctor sense, had ever done him harm. In general they kept themselves to themselves, and only on one occasion had there ever been the slightest trouble – when a Dentist got drunk and, recognizing Lucian Freud, punched him out, saying: 'There, that's for your grandfather.' There they would be at the bar, enjoying their sixty minutes of loose-tied rebellion, and there Josh would be, tucked round the corner and waiting for Cecilia, and that was that. In fact Josh fancied that the Dentists liked having him around, to shoot covert glances at. Who *is* that chap? he imagined them thinking. He certainly looks familiar to me. A movie star perhaps. A writer. A painter. And by Saturday, on their nineteenth hole session in Bird's Custard Land, this would have hardened into certainty: Hey, guess who I saw in my West End drinking club last Wednesday? That actor who played opposite Audrey Hepburn in that film – what was it called? Stocky chap. Thick black hair. Bit foreign looking close to. Keeps himself to himself but seems nice enough ... Josh liked, too, the way the Dentists stirred when Cecilia arrived. Like spooked and skittish pigeons. Christ, he fucks *her* does he? I'd give anything to give her one. Come to think of it, *she* looks a bit familiar, too...

All in all, having the Dentists around made Josh feel pretty good. But he hadn't imagined that one would ever start talking to him. He was the most dentist-looking Dentist of the lot, a man of such ramrod straightness, creased suit-trousers, modest lapels, neatly knotted tie (no loosening here), thickly rimmed spectacles, closely shaved chin and apologetically bumbling voice, that every atom of his being bespoke the highest form of orthodontics. The first time he spoke to Josh he was so diffident that the words scarcely spilled at all from his fastidious lips, and Josh, having had just the one and feeling friendly, dropped off his bar stool and bent an obliging ear to this Dentist of Dentists. 'I didn't catch that,' he said.

'I s-said, what'll you have?' Behind the near-opaque lenses and heavy black frames, the Dentist's eyes fell nervously on Josh's near-empty glass.

Since meeting Dan, Josh drank all sorts, not just beer or rum as he did when he hit Soho. This lunchtime, he had started, for no particular reason, on a combination Cecilia had introduced him to. He shrugged. Never turn down a drink, even if, as at present, his drinking was generally taken care of. 'Kind of you,' he said. 'I'll have a brandy and peppermint.'

The Dentist grinned. 'Do you mind?' He shuffled up his stool so it was adjacent to Josh's. The two men climbed aboard the gondola. Josh sensed suddenly that this was no ordinary Dentist; that drinking, in the sense of a seriously sustained activity that was not merely the adjunct to conversation or the general passing of time but the very essence, for its duration, of being alive, was about to begin. He rubbed his hands and felt thrilled. 'Have you ever tried a Dog's Nose?' said the Dentist.

Josh gazed at the ceiling. Among the gold barrel vaulting, he saw an imaginary prompt mouthing 'No'. He shook his head. 'I don't believe I have,' he said. 'What is it?'

'It's what does the trick,' replied the Dentist. 'Always assuming, of course, that the trick needs doing. Barman,' he went on, suddenly a very assertive sort of Dentist, 'a brace of canine olfactory organs, if you please.'

The barman was the best sort, impassive and choreographed. 'Two house specials?' he said. 'Certainly sir.' He took two pint jugs and, one after the other pulled bitter into them to within a half-inch of the rim. He swivelled, went straight to a stainless steel measure, and plopped two fingers of London gin in the top of each mug. He pushed the mugs across the bar top. Josh and the Dentist looked at each other. The gondola of their ferris wheel had just clicked over. They were poised at the top of the circle. When they looked down they couldn't even see their own feet.

They fell through the afternoon, drinking and talking. For once Cecilia was detained and failed to show up. The Dentists all left, and still they kept on. Reminded by the name Dog's Nose, Josh told this ur-Dentist about Dogboy, his youthful self. The Dentist said Josh was a sailor, he could smell sailors a nautical mile off. Josh insisted he was a poet. The Dentist said he loved sailors. The Dentist closed his pudgy hand over Josh's fist, the one with LOVE on the knuckles. Did Josh know why he loved sailors? Josh asked him politely to remove his hand. 'Here today, gone tomorrow. That's why.' Josh said he had to go. The Dentist asked, begged, Josh to come back to his flat in Bayswater. 'Come and read me some of your poems, sailor boy.'

'Another time,' said Josh.

It would be misleading to suggest that Josh drank exclusively in the Gargoyle. He told me he spent almost as much time in the one-roomed private drinking club in Dean Street known as the Colony Room. I know we have yet to take that narrow, dingy staircase – passing a tart's spent client clattering down – up to 'Muriel's', as it was known. To be honest, I was putting the moment off because the idea of Muriel Belcher, who owned and ran the place, terrifies me. Put it this way, if she managed to put the wind up Deakin (which she did, constantly berating him for his epic stinginess) she'd make mincemeat of me. Deakin photographed Muriel and Bacon painted her, both capturing those laser-beam eyes and raptor's beak of a nose, the black hair pulled back from the forehead and into a bob behind the ears, the imperious tilt of the chin. There she sits, like the figurehead of an icebreaker, on a stool by the door, a sort of divine umpire bestowing sometimes life, sometimes death on the pathetic hopefuls who stumble to her door. Josh she loved, I can see that. She too was an outsider, a bisexual brummie of Portuguese–Jewish parents, who knew nothing, and cared less, about art. But she valued sexual aura and infectious laughter and entertaining descents into drunkenness, and had infallible antennae for pomposity and boringness. To camp comic effect she used 'she' in place of 'he', and outdid most comedians in having not one but several catchphrases: 'Get your bead bag out, Lottie' (to mean bastards like Deakin who didn't buy their round); 'Back to your lovely cottages' (announcing closing time); 'Cunty'. Cunty, for Christ's sake!

I suppose what I fear is following Josh up those sticky linoleum stairs, seeing him duck past Muriel on her stool as she favours him with a rare smile and then have her give me the once-over before consigning me to oblivion: 'She's not a pretty lady is she? On your way Cunty before I give you a fourpenny one.' But I can still take you to Muriel's. The risk-free way is through the eye of artist Michael Andrews, as expressed in his gigantic canvas *The Colony Room*. There they swirl, in sickly submarine light: Bacon from the rear, his hair swept back and overlapping like a bird's wings, talking to a white-faced, jutting-jawed Muriel; by her right shoulder an intense Lucian Freud; by the mirror on the extreme left Jeffrey Bernard; in the left foreground, also from the rear, a seated John Deakin; approaching him, wild-eyed and anxious, con-ceivably paying back an insult from the previous night, a model called Virginia Slater. And behind these *dramatis personae*, the extras – myriad shadowy figures of whom one, doubtless, is Josh. Almost all the chroniclers of the era agree that the Colony Room was quite the place, perhaps because none has wanted to admit that Muriel didn't like them or saw through them. But Dom Moraes, the poet who married Henrietta, remembered chiefly the 'lonely men in corners, staring'. Just remember that; just consider that one of those lonely men may have been Josh.

Deakin came up trumps. In the summer of 1953, having made his mark in the somewhat unlikely setting of *Vogue* as one of the foremost photographers of the day, he obtained a com-mission from the John Player Tobacco Company to produce a series of Player's cigarette advertisements for billboards and point-of-sale displays. After meetings with Player's executives it was agreed that he should use two models, a man and a woman, to promote a modern, egalitarian and healthily outdoor image. For his models he required youth, wholesome good looks, approachability and classlessness. He chose Josh and a model barely out of her teens called Virginia Slater, who features in Michael Andrews's paintings of the Colony Room and would later become the third wife of Michael Law.

It could have been his legendary meanness that made Deakin choose two unknowns for the assignment. Assuming he had negotiated a budget, he presumably stood to pocket any monies saved by hiring cheap models. Virginia recalled that she and Josh made shockingly little for a nationwide advertising campaign. On the other hand, Deakin was a famous perfectionist when it came to his work. Most likely, he felt the use of cheap unknowns would both save him money and give him the look he required, and if he could kill two birds with one stone then why look elsewhere?

There's a curious passage in Dan Farson's autobiography in which he alludes to the Player's assignment and claims it was a catastrophe – that Deakin, having hired Josh and Virginia, proceeded to photograph them using the wrong brand of cigarette as a prop, and that when Player's saw the early results they fired Deakin and found another photographer to do the campaign. It sounds unlikely, despite Deakin's propensity for screwing up his jobs and getting himself sacked, that between them Deakin, Josh and Virginia would have been so stupid as to smoke and brandish, say, Craven As throughout the assignment – especially as Player's had supplied Deakin with a crate of their own brand, with the famous Captain Webb embossed on every packet, to help him along. And in any case there is incontrovertible evidence that the job passed off successfully: I have, in front of me now, three out-takes from the shoot, which took place in Hastings;

I have the finished thing – a cardboard point-of-sale display with a triangular flap at the back to enable it to free-stand on a newsagent's till; and I have the testimony of Virginia Law, née Slater.

Virginia lives with Michael Law and I met her when I visited Michael in their home in south London. Virginia, like Michael and Norman Bowler, said things about Josh that I couldn't digest straight away. We will get to these things soon enough. Meanwhile, I can tell you that the Virginia of 1953 – like Josh, in a belted gaberdine mac – was slim-calved with a dazzling smile and she gazed with something approaching love into Josh's eyes. For Josh it was – the man! – who held the Promised Land, the packet of cigarettes, in his hand. The surviving out-takes are three among probably hundreds of pictures Deakin shot in order to find the handful of usable shots he required. The shoot evidently took place on a stormy and cold day; as I said, Josh and Virginia are both wearing macs and these ripple and ruck like Renaissance marble in a stiff offshore breeze. In one picture they are standing by the hull of a wooden boat; in another, standing on the pier by the railings, clutching each other tight; in the third, the most natural and attractive, paddling in foam at the edge of the sea (Virginia now in a headscarf and still wearing high heels though one foot is covered to the ankle in foamy water). In all of the pictures they are smoking and Virginia has that worshipful expression in her eyes, and in all Josh manages to insinuate, presumably as instructed, a packet of Player's Navy Cut Medium. The wind ruffles his hair and he looks genuinely happy – as well he might, for on that blustery day in Hastings he perhaps believed he was on the edge of something big.

I found the finished article, the cardboard point-of-sale prop, much more interesting than the out-takes, not least because I fancied it might hold at least one clue as to Josh's failure to progress in the male model stakes. It features a head-and-shoulders shot of Josh and Virginia half-sideways on to the camera, gazing lovingly into each other's eyes whilst smoking. Josh's eyes, in particular, are saucer-like, lambent, and the whole image is rather strange, almost other-worldly, because the colour film has been skilfully enhanced here and there with over-painting. The slogan is: 'People love Player's.' But the strange thing is that if Virginia hadn't told me that it was Josh in this advertisement, I probably wouldn't have recognized him. The reason for this is that the shape of his nose has been altered, giving an entirely different cast to his face. It is particularly marked because the photograph catches the profile of the nose. Josh's olfactory organ was a touch bulbous, with something of the ski slope on the bridge. In the Player's ad it is aquiline, as unexceptionably straight and slim as Basil Rathbone's. This shocked me, not just because I thought that tinkering with reality in this way was confined to the computer age, but because it altered so utterly the way Josh looked. Could it be that in the perceived shortcomings of Josh's nose, in errant millimetres of facial flesh, lay the difference between Josh as some sort of advertising ideal and Josh as just another face in the crowd? Why, after all, hire a model whose nose you kept having to paint over afterwards when you could hire a man with the required nasal endowment in the first place?

Whatever the truth of this, the Player's ad. was considered a success. And throughout the summer of 1953 and for a few years to follow, in tobacconists', corner shops, cinemas and garages from Carlisle to Penzance, a nasally modified, wide eyed and smiling Josh became a familiar and reassuring face. It wasn't just the point-of-sale displays, though these seemed more real to me because I had seen one. The 'People love Player's' campaign apparently extended to advertising billboards. Each time I come across a photograph of the period I look past the men in mufflers, the children with moon faces, to scour the hinterlands of the image for a distant, pixilated hoarding. One day I will find him there. Meanwhile, imagine it: on buses and lampposts and old Andersen shelters, at floodlit Molineux as Hancock tore down the wing with the ball glued to his globular bootcap, on the sliced-off sides of bombed out buildings – including one in Dean Street, opposite the entrance to the Gargoyle – Josh's eyes, as blue and gigantic as those of Doctor T.J. Eckleburg in *The Great Gatsby*, staring down.

And who, I wonder, would have paused to consider whether this happy smoker didn't perhaps look familiar, before shaking such madness from their heads and going on their way? The tobacconist in Liskeard, for example, with whom Josh's idealized simulacrum now spent eight hours of every day; an old shipmate; Josh's blowsy, beautiful mother; his bastard of an old man?

DANCERS AT THE GARGOYLE CLUB, 1956, BY THURSTON
HOPKINS (HULTON GETTY)

Chapter 8

'It's in *Our Mutual Friend*!' I saved Louise's message and, every so often, as our appointment drew nearer, I called it up and dwelt upon it. And as time went on, the phrase assumed new and astonishing facets. At first I saw in it merely a gesture of friendliness and sensitivity, a piece of bridge-building I scarcely deserved after the ill-judged and abusive email I had sent her. Though not, let's face it, knowing me terribly well, Louise had evidently figured I was the bookish type, intrigued by arcane trivia and therefore bound to be interested in this literary connection. It was even possible, I reckoned, that she had deliberately chosen this particular pub, the Grapes in Narrow Street, Limehouse, for us to meet in *because* it appeared in Dickens. It would certainly have given us something to talk about, a navigational aid with which to negotiate those first awkward minutes before the drink kicked in. So this is what I assumed initially, and very grateful I was for her thoughtfulness. Already, she had more than compensated for failing to turn up at the French.

But then I delved deeper and discovered there were other resonances to her choice of the Grapes. I dug out my old Penguin edition of *Our Mutual Friend*. I had last opened it while revising for my English degree and in the margins were written, in excessively neat pencil, earnest phrases such as 'river as metaphor!' and 'urbanization, effects of'. In it I discovered that the fictional pub to which Louise must have been referring in her email message was the Six Jolly Fellowship Porters, a red-curtained lopsided tavern 'dropsically bulging' over the slimy, oozing and corpse-strewn Thames at Limehouse. One feels a glow of contentment just reading about the Porters. Outside may be decay and misapprehension, but inside is a bar 'to soften the human breast'. In a space not much larger than a hackney coach are crammed casks and cordial bottles and lemons in nets, and in the corner burns a fire. Next to it are kept tin utensils, shaped like inverted, pointy hats, into which may be poured the specials of the house in order to heat them up in the glowing nooks of the fire. I was skim-reading at this point, but the name of one of the 'delectable drinks' heated up in this manner caught my eye: Dog's Nose. They drank Dog's Nose in the Six Jolly Fellowship Porters, just as they did in the Gargoyle!

Josh, recounting his decades of drinking, particularly remembered the Dog's Nose they served in the Gargoyle (as did war hero and travel writer Paddy Leigh Fermor, who recalled drowning his hangovers 'like kittens' by means of it). Josh was very young in those days, barely an apprentice drinker, but he quickly developed a taste for Dog's Nose. The combined immediate effect of the beer and gin, especially when taken at speed and with a serious hangover, as was the tradition in the Gargoyle, was nigh on miraculous, he recalled: like being struck on each temple simultaneously by very large wooden mallets, or being trapped in the striking mechanism of a town hall clock at noon. The aftermath was scarcely less amazing; a sort of demented mellowness whose peculiar proportions of anxiety and equanimity are captured by Colin MacInnes, author of *Absolute Beginners*, in an article in *Encounter* written in 1957: '... you feel like the fish in the tank above the cash register – swimming aimlessly among artificial water weeds, mindless in warm water.' MacInnes, as a matter of fact, was talking not about the Gargoyle, but the Colony Room, but you get the drift and, in any case, the Colony Room was about to become significant in a way I couldn't have begun to imagine.

I continued reading *Our Mutual Friend*, my senses on red alert since the Dog's Nose reference, and presently I came across this: 'Miss Potterson, sole proprietor and manager of the Fellowship Porters, reigned supreme on her throne, the Bar, and a man must have drunk himself mad drunk indeed if he thought he could contest a point with her.' Miss Abbey Potterson presides over the Six Jolly Fellowship Porters with hauteur and vigilance. Drunken, bleary men are swatted aside. She strides among Captain Joey, Tom Tootle and Jack Mullins as a giant among insects. Sound familiar? The more I read of Abbey Potterson, the more my neck tingled and my palms sweated and, mentally, I doffed my cap to the byzantine subtlety and mental mischief of Louise. For Abbey Potterson *is* Muriel Belcher, proprietress and gorgon of the Colony Room.

Who would have thought that such an apparently simple, innocuous message as Louise's could have contained so much? For having examined this matter from every conceivable direction, I firmly believed her reference to *Our Mutual Friend* and her choice of the Grapes in Limehouse as our point of rendezvous were hugely significant. I had certainly not realized, when I invited her to the French and mentioned her likeness to a certain painterly muse, that Louise would have picked up so sharply my interest in fifties Soho. But pick it up she surely had; and not just picked it up. For now Louise was running with it. Louise was leading me on. And shortly we would meet, and I would discover what she was getting at, what she proposed.

There's a story about the Gargoyle that encapsulates those

feverish times. The nightly party was in full swing, the tiny lift having hauled up its usual catch of odd and exotic fish, when a couple of hoodlums tried to hold the place up at gunpoint. They jammed the lift at the top, tied up the barman and emptied his till, then moved towards the ballroom where they proposed to terrify the revellers into handing over their valuables. Standing at the top of the wide stairs that led on to the dance floor, they waved their revolvers about and shouted 'This is a raid! Everyone down on the floor!' The band played on. Nobody had heard them over the music. Those few who remarked them brandishing their guns passed by with a shrug – they would have to do more than that to get themselves noticed in such a seen-it-all place as the Gargoyle. The exasperated robbers moved down among the crowds of dancing people, yelling and waving their guns with negligible response, until a socialite called Caryl Chance noticed them and said, 'Oh don't be so silly, darlings. You look absolutely lovely and I'm going to dance with you.' As she attempted to embrace them, the police arrived on a tip-off and handcuffed them. Gunmen and police were on familiar, friendly terms. 'I don't believe this lot,' complained one of the robbers. 'I've never seen such disgraceful behaviour in all my life.'

'Ooh I know,' commiserated a copper. 'It's not a place to be.'

The only thing that wasn't tolerated in the evening in the Gargoyle was the mousy and predictable. The Logical Positivist A.J. 'Freddie' Ayer, then the Grote Professor of the Philosophy of Mind and Logic at University College, London, habitually got tight and did the soft shoe shuffle there. Sitting at a dance-floor table, Graham Greene once challenged Ayer to destroy with his famous logical positivism the Catholicism Greene had embraced. 'Between the stirrup and the ground, there is still room and time for me to be damned,' I fancy him telling Ayer with a tilt of his Scotch-on-the-rocks.

Also Gargoyle Club members were Freddie Ayers' old schoolmate, Guy Burgess and Burgess's fellow spook and defector Donald MacLean. Burgess is remembered for having tried to seduce the painter Johnny Minton with an offer of whipping and wine, while MacLean would drink himself to the point of insensibility and then tell anyone within earshot that he spied for Uncle Joe Stalin, a claim which scarcely raised an eyebrow. Two days before Burgess and MacLean defected, on 25 May 1951, Burgess dined at the Gargoyle. In the frenzy of speculation that followed their defection, in particular as to the identity of the other spies in the ring, the practical consideration of how they kept in touch with each other and with their contacts at the Soviet Embassy was never satisfactorily answered. The answer, almost certainly, is that they used the Gargoyle, whose members were unshockable and incurious.

How did Josh fit in to this extraordinary milieu? With both Dan Farson and Cecilia Graye he was little more than a bauble – arm candy, in today's parlance – and that was common enough in the Gargoyle. Servicemen were especially popular, with men and women, in the post-war years. They looked good, their requirements were simple – get drunk and get laid – and they always had a ship or base to return to just when you might start to tire of them. Johnny Minton and bookseller–publisher David Archer were great ones for sailors in particular. Josh was slightly different in that he had deserted and, in addition to the usual requirements, needed somewhere to stay. But in general, and notwithstanding occasional vague rumours that he was a painter or a poet, his youth and looks and his obvious pecuniary reliance on first Dan and then Cecilia put him firmly in the pretty-boy, here today gone tomorrow camp. But then Josh's four-foot-high face was hoisted above Dean Street, and things changed.

From his position above central Soho, Josh's image surveyed the nexus of streets that made up what George Melly called 'that dodgy never-never land, that hallucinatory enclave where we waited, consumed by angst, to cure today's hangover by making certain of tomorrow's.' From his billboard Josh watched himself tumble nightly from the swing doors of the French and, in the company of a giggling, hawking coterie, walk spring-stepped northward, the thick hair that swirled on the crown of his head shining in the lamplight, his laughter carrying into the sky. He watched himself, now directly below, stop to light a cigarette and glance upward at himself, his chums pointing and shouting 'Oi! Got a light up there, cock?', then turn clattering on to the cobbles of Meard Street and thence through the portico of the Gargoyle, or disappear before the Meard Street turning through the Colony Room's dingy aperture on the east side of Dean Street. And, four, five, six hours later, the fog now wrapped yellowly round the moon over Shaftesbury Avenue and the milk carts already clanking down from Warren Street, evening's end: drunks spilling back, like lava, into the streets, no longer discrete individuals but flows of belching; staggering anger and euphoria shouting to the chimney pots, retching through the drain grates, breaking bottles for the hell of it. Josh is always down there somewhere, a link in the chain, an atom of the flow, happy and insensible.

People bought him drinks on the strength of the cigarette ad. A common joke was for someone to offer him a rival brand to Player's, a Craven A or Woodbine, then pretend-withdraw it with a look of horror and a profuse apology: 'But you're a Player's Navy Cut Medium man – I forgot.' And Josh would go along with the joke, tucking the offending cig. behind his ear until such time, he implied, that Player's released him from the yoke of brand identity. Of course the *real* joke about this is that after the flat, derisory modelling fee he received from Deakin for the shoot, Josh got not a penny from Player's. Nowadays he would be bought lock, stock and barrel and turned into a living logo; his looks, together with the modicum of public familiarity that Josh achieved through a nationwide advertising campaign, enough to propel him on to the trash-celeb circuit, and into the money, for a year or two at least. Back then, the reward was less tangible but more precious: self-respect.

With the Player's ad., Josh stopped being a bauble and became a promising artiste. People still weren't quite sure what he did. Was he really a poet, or painter, as someone had told them, who had taken the Player's job for the money (some money!), or was he really a model–actor for whom the advert represented a shrewd career move? At any rate both men and women agreed that he was extraordinarily handsome. Shame, they all said, that he was spoken for, that he was seeing that sexy, dark-haired toff Cecilia.

Unlikely as it may seem, Josh had managed to avoid a direct confrontation with Dan Farson since the moment he gave the fat man the slip in Meard Street several months before. After assiduously dodging him for several weeks, Josh had grown more relaxed about seeing Farson. Several times they had been in the same bar at the same time, and though their eyes had met, their respective journeys to bar or urinal had not coincided and they had never come face to face. It was true that on a couple of occasions recently Dan had made friendly overtures to Josh via Cecilia. Would he care for a drink sometime for old time's sake? Just to let Josh know there were no hard feelings ... Having considered these, Josh had shrugged and decided to do nothing about them. Perhaps Farson was stung by being ignored. At any rate, one night in the Gargoyle he detached himself from his group, which included Francis Bacon, and joined Josh's, which comprised Cecilia, Virginia Slater and a sailor on shore-leave who had clocked Josh's tattoos in the French and invited himself along. Cecilia was waxing mock-indignant about a 'humorous' article she had read in *Picture Post*.

'Don't mention that ghastly comic to me,' said Dan cheerily, by way of introducing himself. Josh and Cecilia ignored him. The sailor looked at them with expectant loyalty, as if awaiting the signal to batter this unwanted arrival.

'I mean, listen to this,' Cecilia continued. She held the magazine to the candle flame in the middle of the table to read from it: ' "The young Englishman is almost as bad a lover as he is a waiter! One suspects because, in both cases, he considers the work beneath him".'

'Beneath him!' sniggered the sailor. 'Too right.'

'The buggers shafted me,' said Farson. 'But don't worry, Mick.' He beamed at Josh, half-extended a consoling arm towards him. 'I blame the donkey. It's strictly donkey business. Remember?' Farson's cackling laugh turned into a paroxysm of coughing, his red face bulged even redder.

The group stared at him, then Cecilia continued: 'Well my point is, I think that's frightfully unfair. Mick is a marvellous lover.' She patted Josh's knee. 'Better than all these put together.' She read again from the magazine: ' "Italian Master: Rudolf Valentino. Smouldering Mexican: Ramon Novarro. French tough: Jean Gabin." You can keep the lot of them, is what *I* say.'

'What about Gregory Peck?' said Virginia Slater. 'Gregory Peck now, I'd take *him* on holiday.'

' "The English Valentino",' said Josh in a mid-Atlantic, MC's voice. He flung out a hand, writing the slogan against the gold vaulting of the ceiling. 'P'raps that's what I'll be. I like that.'

'More like the Spanish Fly,' said Farson, winking at Josh, who ignored him.

'D'you know,' said Cecilia, frowning and reading, 'when

Valentino died, fifteen women committed suicide? That's what it says.'

Farson had been smiling and nodding, trying desperately to be noticed and included. His face shone with sweat. He'd had several too many and his judgment was shot. Now he leant forward and said, smiling: 'Yes, isn't Mick a marvellous lover? I thought so too. So considerate – and ...', he looked at the ceiling searching for the right word, '... inventive.'

'Leave it,' said Josh, finally looking directly at his erstwhile would-be lover. 'Just piss off back to your own table.'

Cecilia stared at Farson. 'You're wrong,' she said, 'if you think I care a fig for what you say.'

The sailor brought his fist down on the table and the candle toppled over and died in its own wax.

Above the din, Farson ploughed on: 'Or should I say, invented? Because that's what he is. That's what you are, isn't it Mick? I made him up. Go on, ask him where he comes from. Ask him where he got that suit he's wearing. The way he speaks! Pretty boy Michael – pah! I invented him.'

Josh held up his left fist with HATE on it and showed it first to Farson and then to the sailor. The sailor scraped back his chair, swivelled his body and cocked his leg, and delivered to Farson's chest a kick that was like the half-cycle of a piston. Farson flew backwards and landed back among his own group. 'Thanks, I'll have another brandy and peppermint,' said the sailor, realigning and relighting the candle.

'Girls, *really*!' said Francis Bacon, putting on a show of disapproval. 'It's *too* bad.'

Did Henrietta remember him, when *she* finally ran into Josh? Or did she simply fancy the man whose billboard eyes followed her up and down Dean Street? Josh told me that at the time it didn't cross his mind that she might not recall the figure who had pursued her, skulked in doorways on the off-chance of running into her. But thinking about it long afterwards, it struck him that she may well not have known who he was, for a great deal of both drink and men was passing her lips that summer. At any rate, she came up to him one night in the Gargoyle, when Cecilia was away from his table, and suggested they went to the Ladies for a fuck. He was particularly tickled by the invitation as she adduced, as further encouragement, the particularly fine fittings and layout of the ladies' lavatories. They were spacious, she said. The cubicle doors, and dividing partitions, were of heavy mahogany. The brass handles gleamed. It would be like making love in the captain's cabin of the Queen Mary – without the rocking movement of course, but they could supply that themselves. Josh grinned as he allowed her to tug him to his feet. She dance-stepped across the floor, pulling him astern.

People watched. Bacon watched, not directly, but in the pieces of mirror on the walls. Those shards of silver-backed glass mirrored the function of his paintings: they pulled people to bits and stuck them back together in ways you would not have thought of. The minute vertical discrepancies from piece to piece exposed the hilarious dislocation of things. Bacon found the Gargoyle particularly good for picking up the gossip and insight on other people's lives that made him glad to be alive. Had he marked Josh out by this point? The answer is almost certainly yes, for Josh was of the type – rough, physical, untutored – if not the sexual orientation that Francis was to go for all his life. And they had, of course, already met. At any rate, he watched, via the wall, the fractured images of Henrietta tugging Josh across the dancefloor; saw them climb the shallow flight of stairs that led to the lift and the lavatories; saw them return, separately, some ten minutes later, dispersing to different parts of the ballroom; and made a natural assumption about what they had been up to. It tickled him to think it, especially when he saw Cecilia presently join Josh and drape herself around him, lighting cigarettes for them both and placing one carefully between his lips. But Francis was wrong about what had happened. Had the light been higher, he would have seen the tears of rage glistening in Henrietta's eyes when she returned, and realized she hadn't been fucked at all, or at least not in the way she had planned.

Josh was cocky that summer. The days moved on, reaching the blowsy and overblown state. He still believed things could last forever; he was still on his bike, dogs bouncing alongside him, heading for a tumble. The first thing to happen was that Cecilia left, and I can't help wondering whether everything else that happened wasn't made inevitable by this unfortunate circumstance, for Cecilia was his rudder, and for twenty-five years after they parted he would drift, until he met Jean. There was no bad feeling in their split. Cecilia's parents returned from their spring gambling binge, poured cold water on their daughter's stated ambition to be a photographer and packed her off to her cousin in Vermont, with a Swiss finishing school lined up for the autumn. There were tears, chiefly from her, on their last night together. She promised fervidly that she would run away, back to London, to be with him; and Josh made a somewhat half-hearted reciprocal promise, presenting the possibility that they would cross in mid-ocean. But, initially at least, Josh felt her absence most keenly in respect of suddenly having nowhere to stay.

He solved this easily enough by picking up women in one or other of his Soho haunts and returning home with them. In general they were older than him because older women were more likely to have their own places. Often they were married and the husbands absent. Josh admitted he was pretty indiscriminate and ruthless at this time. He would dump a girl as soon as he had found her if someone prettier, or richer came along. He slept with the wives and girlfriends of men he knew. He was drinking too much, he got the clap and passed it on without a thought. Some of his fellow drinkers began to hope to see him brought down a peg or two. In particular, Dan and Henrietta would narrow their eyes a fraction when they heard or sensed his presence. Perhaps someone even tipped off the police that a deserter was on the loose (and, the informant may have added, had had the cheek to have his face enlarged several hundred times, duplicated several thousand, and then emblazoned the length and breadth of the country). But Josh never did discover the truth about that.

Josh, then, was heading for a fall. But even then, twixt stirrup and ground, he had the chance to save himself. And if what follows is true, Josh had no right to enquire of Norman Bowler, many years later, 'What went wrong?' To tell him plaintively, 'I could have been you.'

Michael Law remembered that a regular in the Gargoyle that summer was the American film director George Stevens, who the previous year had made the classic Western *Shane* with Alan Ladd. Perhaps it was Stevens who one evening invited fellow American filmmaker Raoul Walsh to the Gargoyle. At any rate, Walsh went and, if the story is to be believed, spotted Josh and decided he wanted the feller with the jet hair and killer looks in the movie he was then casting for.

The story of the Raoul Walsh film comes not from Josh – he never mentioned it to me – but from a drinking friend of Josh's called Frank from his later, Hampstead days. I remembered Frank belatedly. On my childhood visits to Greensands Frank would occasionally turn up, having walked across the fields from Steyning with his dogs. His trademark was the quarter-bottle of whisky he stashed in the hood of his waxed jacket as he walked. Josh and Frank had been on some heavy-duty drinking adventures together, that much I had gathered.

I remembered Frank as a cheeky Londoner type, always with a drink in his hand and a story on the go. Well, when I met him, having found to my surprise that he was still in the phone book and given him a call, he was seven eighths of the way to his grave. But he still had a drink in his hand.

I had arranged to meet him in a pub in Steyning and was driving slowly up the high street when I thought I saw him on the other side of the road: tubbier, balder, greyer, but recognizably Frank. I slowed the car and yelled from the window. He turned and stared at me in puzzlement. He hadn't a clue who I was. 'We're supposed to meet,' I explained. 'In ten minutes. At the pub.'

'Are we?' he shrugged. 'OK.' So he came over and I drove him the final hundred yards. Evidently he had completely forgotten our telephone conversation, during which he had assured me he remembered me from Greensands in the seventies. In fact, throughout our strange meeting he behaved as if he didn't know me from Adam. It was just luck that I had driven past him on the way to our supposed meeting, though no doubt he would have dropped into the pub at some stage. Still, he was more than happy to have an excuse for a drink, especially if someone else was paying.

I bought him a double vodka and we sat in the garden next to a wooden climbing frame, the only customers at this early hour on a weekday. As he took his first sip and fumbled for his cigarettes, he told me cheerfully that his doctor had told him he'd be dead in three months if he didn't lay off the booze. I planted a second drink in front of him and prompted him about Josh, and, like a one-armed bandit, he clicked and whirred and obliged with stories of their Hampstead days. It was the usual stuff about drinking and fighting. Hetta Empson, with whom Josh was then sleeping, off and on, was always attacking him – with a broken bottle or a heavy ashtray – and he was forever turning up at their favourite pub, the

Rosslyn Arms, covered in blood. One story struck a chord, though. Josh had got into a fight in a restaurant and been arrested and bound over to keep the peace. When the story appeared in the *Hampstead & Highgate Express*, Josh was described as a poet. 'He loved it,' said Frank. 'The thought of being a poet. He was always telling people at Hetta's he was a poet. But then he'd come unstuck sometimes 'cos he'd meet a real poet. Then Hetta would say something like, "Oh don't worry, he's an absolute poet in bed and that's all that matters," and of course no one dared take Josh on 'cos he could handle himself. Of course,' Frank added, lighting up another cig, 'what he could have been was a film star, if he hadn't been such an idiot.' And then Frank told me the story of Raoul Walsh.

Not that he knew the director's name, or the name of the film. All he remembered was that the star was Rock Hudson and that the part that had been Josh's for the taking went instead to a young unknown called Bryan Forbes. It was I who filled in the gaps later, and it all made sense. There had indeed been a film made that year starring Hudson and Forbes. It was *Sea Devils*, directed by Raoul Walsh and – here was the interesting bit – it was described in one of the film reference books as 'a shipbound Napoleonic swashbuckler'. Who better to play a sabre-slashing sea devil than the naval deserter himself?

Walsh had lost his right eye while filming a Western in the Arizona desert – a jack rabbit had come hurtling through the windscreen of his pick-up – and wore a black eyepatch over the socket. He wore hand-made English boots and smoked hand-made cigarettes, thin as drinking straws. Perhaps it was Josh's waistcoat that caught his eye, for Walsh, too, shopped in the Burlington Arcade when he came to London. (The waistcoat, let it be said, was well the worse for wear by now, but in the gloom of the Gargoyle, the peacocks still strutted.)

Or perhaps it was the overall impression Josh made – the hair, the eyes, the cocky lope, what Michael Law described, with Josh in mind, as 'the Sicilian fisherman look'. At any rate, Josh was happy to be summoned by the big American with the pirate's eyepatch, the hands like hams, and the deep voice that managed to sound both avuncular and sinister. They chatted about the film and Josh told him he came from a fishing family in Cornwall, knew all about boats and had sturdy sea legs. Walsh said he had a particular part in mind for Josh, but if he didn't make that there were other, lesser roles for which he would also be well suited. Walsh told Josh to attend an interview at the Dorchester with the casting director. They parted on the best of terms. Josh returned to his table and said to his companion: 'The English Valentino! I knew it.'

But Josh blew it, and I blame Henrietta.

FRANCIS BACON BY DANIEL FARSON (ESTATE OF DANIEL FARSON)

Chapter 9

Emboldened by the ease with which I had tracked down Frank, I thought I'd see if Cecilia could be found. Josh talked about her ever so fondly. They weren't together long but of all the people he met in Soho, she was the nicest, he'd said. Whatever happened to Cecilia? Josh hadn't known, though he supposed that in time she would have settled down with a man of means and lived in New England and the Upper West Side, or Belgravia and the Cotswolds, and perhaps had an affair with her country gardener, partly from boredom and partly from her blithe sense of disorder. This being a sensible assumption, I had no expectation of ever finding her, but I tried the London phone directory anyway. It was a good hunch. There was one entry with the unusual spelling of Graye. The initial was C, and the address was in SW3: 23 Renfrew Apts, Lower Sloane Street. It sounded about right.

I had been busy inducing disorder in the little bedroom-cum-office where I worked, generally making it look more artily messy than it usually did. This counted as a displacement activity. The thing I was trying to displace from my mind was the thought that the next day I was going to meet Louise in the Grapes. I could hardly believe the day had come round already. Louise seemed as unbearably excited as I – she had emailed not once but twice in the previous twenty-four hours, checking I hadn't forgotten, confirming time and place. When

I anticipated the possible events of the next few hours, my mind ran away with me, however hard I tried to rein it in. We meet, we click, we run back to the country together! Hence the desk untidying, the apparently random but pleasing clutter, for when she popped her head round the door on the inspection of the cottage which, glass in hand and shoes kicked off, she would insist on undertaking. To tell you the truth, I was terrified to meet her, would have preferred not to. Anticipation is much better. But it was too late.

The appointment with Louise at the Grapes was not until early evening, so I decided to go up to town early and check out Renfrew Apartments beforehand. I was struck with a general reluctance to meet people, and didn't feel up to actually making myself known to Cecilia − if, indeed, that's who it was − but the idea was to get a good look at her. Anyway, I drove up the A3 and parked near the embankment at Putney. On Putney Bridge I caught a twenty-two bus to Sloane Square, where I alighted while the bus was still moving, a sign, this, of my rising excitement, crossed over to the south side of the square and walked down Lower Sloane Street. On the west side of the street rose towering cliffs of rust-red brick surmounted by chimney stacks as slim as cigarette cases. High up on the brick frontage, Renfrew Apartments advertised themselves in the stylish twenties lettering of French metro stations, an effect somewhat spoiled by the letter p of Apart-ment, which had swung down and now hung from a point at the base of the descending stroke so it read as a solitary letter d. This pretty much summed up the air of delapidated gentility that clung to the mansions. They were stolid and discreet, with stone balustrades and the occasional flourish of a gryphon or dragon on the architraves. Several bore the white heraldic shield of the Banham burglar alarm company. But some of these shields were so old they gave the London telephone number as 01-. Few of the balustrades had window boxes and the brass letter boxes were unpolished. Behind the net curtains and the aspidistra, old ladies who had been debutantes and land girls ate tinned soup and watched daytime television with rugs on their knees. I could not have invented a more appropriate milieu for Cecilia de Becket Graye to live out her days in.

Renfrew Apartments had several entrances. The one giving access to number twenty-three had a bootscraper in the porch with the bulk and presence of an old steam iron, and a chandelier hanging in the hallway. I hovered for a while, peering into the hallway as if Cecilia might suddenly appear there, a faded beauty, a reminder of grander days. My hand kept moving towards the bank of door buzzers then lifting away from it. Finally, feeling as if an air bubble was trapped in my windpipe, I pressed firmly on twenty-three. I stared at the intercom grille, as if I might actually see her words float from it when she spoke ... if she spoke. I waited and waited but the intercom did not crackle to life. I was on the point of leaving, had shifted my thoughts from Cecilia to the forthcoming rendezvous with Louise, when the grille gave a sort of cough, and a thin and metallic voice said: 'Yee-es?'

I stared in horror at the grille, frozen by indecision.

'Hello?' said the voice. 'Is anybody there?'

I leant into the grille. 'Hello,' I stammered. 'Is that – is that Miss Graye?'

Silence. I stared afresh at the grille. My heart beat painfully. The grille coughed again. 'Yee-es,' said the voice. 'Who is this?'

'Parcel for you,' I muttered.

'Eh?' said Cecilia. 'I can't hear you.'

It was her! 'Parcel,' I repeated, then scuttled back down the front steps. I ran two doors along, climbed the steps and hid behind the porch pillars there. By leaning out a fraction I had good views of the entrance to Cecilia's block, should she appear. I waited a good ten minutes, again to the point when I was about to leave. Then I heard a latch click and a door creak slowly open. I did not actually see her. I did not dare risk leaning out too far. But I did see the brim of a straw hat bob briefly into view. Suddenly my subterfuge seemed to me absurd, if not downright mad. Why had I not simply called her on the telephone, explained my interest and arranged a meeting? The answer was that reality was beginning to disappoint me, which is why, notwithstanding my excitement, I also had genuine misgivings about meeting Louise – much better to keep people in the realm of invention, where you can have them pretty much as you wish. What might Cecilia have told me about Josh, for instance? That he wasn't a good lover, or that he treated her badly? It was very possible. I'd had enough cold water poured over me already by his so-called friends from that time.

'He was a sad man,' Norman Bowler had said of Josh. 'There was a dark side to him. There was a dark side to Soho.' Oh yes, I've got that. I keep being dragged there. 'All the people around him,' Norman had gone on, 'were producing – painting, writing, directing – and it must have been frustrating when you weren't.' Got that, too. I wanted Josh to romp through the summer of 1953, stampeding after dustbins and jewels, but that would have meant him eluding the fate that awaited them all. Like Dan, I had made the mistake of thinking I owned Josh, or had partly invented him. But the real Josh kept coming through. Michael Law, for instance, remembered him as a much more passive type than I would have wished for. 'He had the manner of being half asleep all the time. Pink cheeks, heavy eyebrows, lambent eyes. Dozing away in his chair, waiting to be carried off to bed. The looks that women go for. The Sicilian fisherman look which Johnny Minton was also fond of. He had no motivation, he simply went towards what he liked.' Virginia

Law went further. She recalled someone who'd 'had the stuffing knocked out of him. He was wanting to be picked up, looked after. Most people of that age go out and get what they want.' I had so much wanted him to go and get what he wanted, but he *would* go the other way and I couldn't help feeling it would end badly.

What I am saying is that I'd had enough of undiluted reality. The last thing I felt like, especially on the day I was due to meet Louise, was a decrepit Cecilia pouring poison in my ear, so I did not confront her on her porch. But I had plenty of time before my appointment with Louise, and after the tantalizing glimpse of the straw hat I felt sufficiently curious to hang around Renfrew Apartments in the hope of a further view of Cecilia. I paced up and down Lower Sloane Street, I went round the block a couple of times, and eventually my patience was rewarded. Just as I was passing her front gate on yet another patrol, the door opened and the straw hat emerged. The hat was certainly the dominant feature of her appearance, as if she were the subject of a painting entitled *Woman in Hat* whose facial features are entirely subordinate to her headwear. Not only was the brim wide, casting her face into shadow, but a cream coloured silk bandana fell from the bole of the hat across one side of her face and she wore comically large, wraparound sunglasses. In other words, I could gain virtually no sense of what she looked like, beyond the heavily powdered tip of a pretty average sort of nose. Her ensemble almost made up for this disappointment, however. In addition to the hat, she wore another silk scarf up high around her neck, and a jacket of café au lait-and-cream checks whose sleeves were stylishly rolled and whose boxy shoulders bore up the frail and stooped body within. Below baggy silk cream pants she had on spangly gold socks and gold buckled flatties. I could not have made a better job of this outfit had I been inclined to invent it.

In order to take all this in I had resorted to that hackneyed surveillance smokescreen, pretending to tie my shoelaces. As Cecilia closed the gate, turned north and set off towards Sloane Square, I decided to follow, with no particular purpose in mind beyond the thrill of observing someone who doesn't know they are being watched. What I hadn't bargained for was just how slowly old people walk. Cecilia inched her way along the street. I crossed over, pretended to scan the properties in an estate agent's window. After a minute or two I looked back, expecting to see her disappearing into the maelstrom of people that swirled in the square, but she seemed scarcely to have moved ten feet. Eventually, though, after I had visited the WH Smith's on the square, gone to the underground station to check on the price of a ticket and the best route to Canary Wharf, and bought tuna and sweetcorn in a baguette at the mini store there, Cecilia had reached the centre of the square, a little garden sheltered by knobbly-trunked plane trees. Here she slumped on a bench, between a fountain of a nymph holding a conch shell, a statue of Sir Hans Sloane whom acid rain had deprived of the tip of the nose, and a stone drinking fountain erected by the Metropolitan Drinking Fountain and Cattle Trough Association. I sat on a bench not ten feet away and munched my baguette while trying to get a better view of Cecilia's face. This proved difficult. Head down, she rummaged for ages in the hessian bag she carried before pulling from it a pale blue packet. She fiddled with the silver wrapping at the end of the packet and drew from it, with the fastidiousness of tweezers, a cigarette. She lit the cigarette, inhaled deeply and held the smoke, and when she came to exhale lifted her head to the sky so that, for the first time, I saw that she wore lipstick, deep red and thickly applied – the burning cigarette she now held was already rimmed with it. There was something familiar in all of this, though for the moment I could not place it.

I was slowly getting into Cecilia's rhythm. After a leisurely smoke she was off again. At first I thought she was headed for the Peter Jones department store, but her goal was the bus stop outside it, the stop where I had got off from Putney Bridge. I waited alongside her, peering down on the crown of her hat, noticing an errant strand of grey hair which every so often, in an absent-minded gesture, she attempted to prod back under the brim. When the bus came − another twenty-two − I sat behind her on the lower deck, gazing on the tender lozenge of neck between scarf and hat brim which became visible whenever she leaned forward slightly. This bit of neck, I decided, could well have belonged to a woman forty years younger than Cecilia. I imagined Josh stroking it. There was a moment of panic when the conductor asked for my fare and I realized I had no idea where we were bound. But I settled on 'All the way', wherever that was, and sat back to enjoy the ride.

Josh never made it to the Dorchester for his film audition. Something happened in the Gargoyle shortly after he met Raoul Walsh which prevented him. The origin of this event is to be found in the Ladies lavatory the night that Henrietta dragged Josh there for a swift cubicle fuck. The Gargoyle was an enlightened place. Many clubs are enclaves of hidebound snobbery but the Gargoyle was blind to who and what you were and never judged people or actions except insofar as they might be boring or boorish. Having sex in the lavatories was a rare but not unheard-of occurrence, and nobody would have dreamt of complaining about it. But it wasn't sex that took place between Henrietta and Josh that night. It was something like what follows.

She bundled him into the cubicle and slid the bolt behind them. She hitched up her skirt and tugged at his trousers. She manoeuvred him round as if they were in a dancefloor clinch until she could sit on the lavatory seat. Now she worked with absorption on the front of his trousers, biting her lower lip as she tried to prise open the fly buttons and massaging, as she did so, the bulge beneath. She frowned as she rubbed. She had meant the genie of his trousers to grow magically at her touch, but there was no discernible movement in there at all. 'Don't be tense,' she said. 'No one'll hear us. Or if they do they won't mind.' And she took one of his hands and placed it on one of her breasts. 'Enjoy me,' she said. Josh let his hand fall back to his side and looked down impassively as she released the last of his fly buttons. She plunged in her hand and rummaged, narrowing her eyes in a puzzled way at him as she did so. She produced his flaccid penis. 'For God's sake,' she said. 'Are you mad?'

'Perhaps,' he said, and bent his knees, adopting his public urinator's stance.

Well, Josh wasn't proud of this moment. On the other hand, he wasn't ashamed. You used what you had at the time, as he kept saying, and at the time pissing on Henrietta seemed a good way of paying her back. Paying her back for what, precisely, I wanted to know? Failing to be infatuated with him as he was, briefly, with her? Grabbing his cock in the French? But he'd enjoyed that. 'Leading me on then discarding me,' he said. 'They all did. She was just the one that copped it.' The story she told was that he had sexually assaulted her, one assumes because it was too humiliating to admit that he had urinated on her. She did nothing about it that night, passing up the option of making an immediate, official complaint that would have seen Josh barred from the Gargoyle at the very least. Perhaps this was because, given her reputation, she feared she couldn't make such a complaint stick. But in any case she wanted sweeter, bloodier revenge. It was not difficult to get people on her side and against Josh, for, as I have said, he was beginning to put various people's backs up that summer. She wanted him taught a lesson, she said, and that meant only one thing: a good beating. Dan in particular relished the idea of Josh being on the receiving end for once. Francis Bacon was also intrigued, though he hardly knew Josh and certainly felt no personal animus towards him. No, for Bacon, Henrietta's plan was a piece of choreography woven from human madness, and there was nothing he liked more. He had seen the opening steps of the dance and wished for a ringside seat when the performance reached its fist-whirling climax. Effete and pudgy palmed, none of Henrietta's regular drinking crew were up for jumping Josh. What they needed was outside help, and they knew where to get it from.

Johnny Minton loved his sailors. He danced like a dervish while they drank his cider and rum, and if he was lucky one would go back with him to his little house in Apollo Place, Chelsea, and if he was unlucky he would get rolled as he snored afterwards. But he always went back for more. Henrietta chose two big, affable brutes. She knew what poison to drip in their ears. See that man? she said, shouting over the noise of parping trombones as Josh drank and laughed at the bar, one arm draped on a woman's slim shoulders. He's a disgrace to the Senior Service. A deserter and fraud, a womanizer and embezzler. He *this* and he *that* ... Oh, and if they ever wanted a bit of the *other* – she winked, and the matelots looked at each other with glazed eyes as she ordered Johnny to buy them another bottle of rum.

They were drunk when it happened and so was Josh, which resulted in some comical flailing before the real blows landed. They ambushed him as he left the lift at the bottom, having raced down the fire escape on a signal from Henrietta. Like a bottle being shaken dry, the club emptied of its late night drinkers as word got about that a brawl was in progress in Meard Street. It was Buster Keaton stuff at first, and the crowd applauded each missed punch and lost footing. But once Josh was down on the cobbles, there was no getting up, and the crowd closed in, those at the ringside evolving from spectators into aggressors as they realized he couldn't fight back. People got their own back for all sorts of slights, real and imagined. Dan was there, of course, stabbing his heel repeatedly into Josh's shoulder. Henrietta watched the mêlée with satisfaction, then slunk away into the night. Even Francis joined in, contributing rather ladylike toe-pokes to Josh's curled back before realizing his heart wasn't in it and melting back to the edge of the crowd, where he waited eagerly for the blood. And there was blood.

To Francis, life was about man's brutishness, the blood and gristle and pumping viciousness just below the surface; and then, when we are dead, the carcasses we become, and never mind about the soul. Here, in the vermilion and cerise spatterings across the lamplit Meard Street cobbles and the bloody gurglings from Josh's kicked-in mouth, Francis felt the heightened experience of what he called the spasm between two voids. He sat on the steps of number five Meard Street and waited till the thing burned itself out.

People drifted off until only Josh and the two sailors remained. From somewhere, Josh found a second wind, staggered to his feet, backed his way into a corner and raised his fists, which he moved in a whirring motion when the sailors moved in. 'Come ong theng,' he said through the blood and broken teeth. 'You shug be ashaged of yourselves. I was a Buttung Boy for Chrise sake.'

The sailors looked at each other. They panted heavily and the fight had gone out of them. 'Everyone was a fucking Button Boy, if you believe 'em,' said one. 'You can't move for fucking Button Boys.'

'HMS Ganges,' said Josh. 'Look i' up. Michael Avery. HMS Ganges, nin'een for'y eight.'

'I've had enough of this,' said one of the sailors.

'Oh do go home girls,' called Francis from the other side of Meard Street. 'You've had your good run ashore.'

The sailors turned. 'Who the fuck are you?'

'I'm the ship's biscuit. Now on your way or I'll give you a fourpenny one.'

One sailor moved towards Francis, the other dragged him away. 'Let's just go.'

'Where?'

'Anywhere but here.' They lurched off into Dean Street.

'Cheerio!' cried Francis after them. He and Josh eyed each other across the battlefield. Josh was now slumped against the wall, regaining his breath, spitting blood from his mouth. Francis smoothed back his hair with an automatic hand and waited. Eventually Francis said: 'I've lost nearly all my teeth to friends.' He stepped across the street, his boots clip-clopping on the cobbles, and handed Josh his handkerchief. 'It's Mick the painter, isn't it?' Francis was wearing his leather trenchcoat over a double breasted suit. He opened the coat and said, 'Look!' he dropped his suit trousers to his knees. Beneath he wore black lacy knickers, stockings and a garter belt. He allowed Josh time to take in this extraordinary sight, then hitched his trousers back up. 'There it is,' he said.

Josh stared, then began to laugh. His back slid down the wall until he sat in the gutter, and still he couldn't stop laughing. He used Francis' hanky to wipe away the tears of laughter and the blood that continued to bubble from his mouth. 'Steady,' said Francis, 'we don't want you looking too clean. Not yet.'

Footfalls echoed on the cobbles. They turned to see a policeman framed by the lights of Dean Street. 'Don't you ever learn?' said the policeman.

'It's all right, officer,' said Francis. 'I'll take him home. We're all right.'

*

Dan Farson writes in his autobiography that Francis didn't like Josh at all: 'Francis Bacon was immune to his charms, largely because Johnson took no interest in him.' This, from what I was able to make out, is the opposite of the truth, though of course it is true that Josh wasn't interested in Francis sexually. Let's go back to the beginning. Josh and Francis first met in the Gargoyle late at night – that much Josh and Farson agreed on though Josh's version, as described at the beginning of this narrative, is very different from Farson's. Farson places Josh at the head of several tables pushed together, around which are sitting Farson, Johnny Minton, with his great sad Dali's clock of a face, several sailors on shore-leave and in uniform, and some art students from the Royal College of Art, where Minton taught. Minton – who was famously generous and had supplied all the bottles cluttering the tables – is getting drunk and maudlin and eventually comes out with his favourite self-pitying line: 'People only love me because I'm rich.' One of the sailors mutters that Minton has reached the dangerous and tedious stage. 'I can buy anyone I want,' Minton goes on to declare, as if to confirm the truth of the sailor's observation, though he could not buy an antidote to the self-loathing that four years later would lead to his suicide by overdose.

At an adjacent table sit Francis and his lover Peter Lacy, the former Battle of Britain pilot. Farson says the two are in the midst of an angry argument, which makes sense considering Francis' description of his relationship with Lacy as 'four years of continuous horror, with nothing but violent rows.' Josh spots them and, bored with proceedings at his own table, decides to make himself at home at theirs though he has not been introduced. Josh's drunken intervention and unwonted familiarity outrages Bacon, according to Farson. After Josh finally gets the message and leaves Bacon and his boyfriend to it, Farson feels obliged to go over and apologize for his new friend's behaviour, even to the point of paying for Bacon and Lacy's drinks, a foolishly generous gesture which leaves Farson penniless and means he and Josh will have to walk back to Beauchamp Place rather than take a cab as Farson has planned (note the subtly self-serving kilter of this detail).

In other words, Farson has Bacon behave more like a Dentist from Bird's Custard Land than the half-schoolboy, half-satyr (Allen Ginsberg's description) we know him to have been. Of course Josh didn't have the detailed apparent-recall of Dan. All he could remember was coming out with the line about being a painter. At that time, just after his desertion, he was careful not to blab about jumping ship and he said the first thing that came into his head when Francis asked what he did, based on his father's part-time summer work in Liskeard. He admitted that he didn't have a clue who Francis was – he didn't have much of a clue about anything, he said – but that was not the same thing as not being interested in Francis. In fact he had taken to Francis immediately, and Francis had taken to him.

Francis was a man who wore a garter belt beneath a Savile Row Suit beneath a Nihilist's coat, an intellectual who spent much of his time with intellectuals yet professed to be bored by them, and whose work sprang from his nervous system and not from his brain. By and large he preferred the company of crooks and gamblers, drifters, chancers, men on the run – people who would have taken Vorticism to be a venereal disease. In the 1960s Bacon would fall in love with an unsuccessful petty crook from the East End called George Dyer, who had a speech impediment and a prison record. Dyer was the subject of many Bacon paintings. Though he cared nothing for art he was very proud of being painted and would insist on attending exhibition openings and, through a mouthful of glottal stops and dropped aspirates, point his painterly self out to art world bigwigs. In 1971 Dyer died of an overdose of drink and drugs in a hotel in Paris, on the eve of one of Bacon's greatest exhibitions, at the Grand Palais.

Not that Josh was a crook or a Philistine, despite Farson's efforts to paint him so. But he was a young man without home or money and, on the evening Bacon took him back, with a broken nose and injured pride. Bacon himself would have been forty-three but looked a decade younger so people said, which may be accounted a miracle given his unrestrained lifestyle revolving around drink, masochistic sex and punishing work routines. At last his ground-breaking, uncompromising paintings were regarded as among the very finest on the contemporary scene, both in Britain and abroad, and sold for a great deal of money. He spent his money on fine clothes, champagne and oysters and could be massively generous to friends whilst also being suspicious of hangers-on. But he lived a peripatetic and frugal domestic existence at this time, moving between various rented rooms-with-studios in Chelsea and Kensington. It was to one of these – Johnny Minton's mews house in Apollo Place, just off the Chelsea Embankment – that he returned with Josh the night Josh got jumped and bloodied by the sailors.

He made Josh stop under a street light in Wardour Street. The bridge of Josh's nose was already swelling up. Blood still welled into his mouth from the gum sockets of a couple of teeth that now lay somewhere among the Meard Street cobbles. 'How do I look?' said Josh.

'Glittering,' said Francis. 'Oh yes,' he added when Josh rolled his eyes. 'A caved-in mouth has compensations. To be precise, the glitter and colour that comes from an open mouth when a light shines in it. Especially a mouth full of blood.'

'Do you mind?' said Josh.

'Francis will make it all right, I promise,' said Francis. 'Trust her. It's just that I've got a thing about open mouths.

It started with a book. Are you listening? Am I driving you mad with my twitterings? Or do they soothe away the pain? Let us walk and I will soothe you.' And so they walked through the London night, Francis with his characteristic side-to-side gait – as if, as someone remarked, he walked permanently on the deck of a rolling ship – Josh dragging his feet and dripping blood. The city streets were less furred up by neon and parked cars and traffic than they are now. Josh and Francis sailed endless dark blue rivers that seemed to bear them effortlessly on.

'Why are you helping me?' asked Josh as they neared Hyde Park Corner.

'Because,' said Francis.

'I'm not, you know – interested. If that's what you think.'

'Because you live life,' said Francis. 'Because, like me, you think only too much is enough. Is it true?'

Josh shrugged. 'I just go at it,' he said. 'I don't think about it.'

'That's true,' said Francis. 'I believe that's true. You know, to get back to that book, I found it, it must be twenty or more years ago now, in a bookshop in Paris. A book of diseases of the mouth, with beautiful hand-coloured plates, beaut-i-ful, and your mouth just reminded me of it. You made my day! It's not easy to please Francis.' Josh said nothing. After a while, as they passed between the tall apartment blocks of Sloane Street, Francis resumed: 'Where do we come from, do you think?'

'Cornwall,' mumbled Josh. 'I come from Cornwall.'

'Hah! Before Cornwall. I'll tell you. Nothing. And where do we go to?'

'Nothing?' said Josh.

'*Nada,*' confirmed Francis. 'How does that make you feel?'

'It makes my mouth sore,' said Josh. 'It makes my nose feel like a football.'

'Oh look!' exclaimed Francis. 'I swear you're sprinkling star dust on the evening.' They were approaching a road junction. Across the road, on the far pavement, shimmered a pool of fresh blood beneath a cone of street light. The pool was fed by a crimson stream that, obeying the immutable laws of liquid in motion, imitated the coils of a mighty river as it flowed from the shadows of a hedgerow bordering a private garden. Francis shot across the road ahead of Josh, stepped carefully around the blood, and bent down to peer into the shadows under the hedge. 'It's a dog!' he reported back excitedly. He bent lower, reached out gingerly and touched the dog. 'Oh my,' he breathed. 'It's dead. And it glitters. See, Mick, how it glitters.'

Josh had reached the middle of the road. He groaned, averting his face. 'Come away. I can't stand it.'

'Oh but you've got to look,' said Francis. He picked up the dog's hind legs and began to drag it from the shadows where it had been thoughtful enough to hide before dying. The dog lay on its side. Its uppermost flank had been split open, as if by a deep and careful incision, although presumably a car had been responsible. The split skin gaped. From this gaping wound, like fruit in a jelly, bulged the dog's viscera.

Josh crossed to the west side of the street and said. 'For Christ's sake leave it alone. I'm going. This is not right.' He began to walk briskly away towards Sloane Square.

Francis scarcely noticed him leave, so fascinated was he by the dead dog. He spat on his hands, breathed deeply for Dutch courage and carefully dragged the dog backward towards the cone of light thrown by the street lamp. He arranged the dog's gaping wound in the centre of the light and stepped back to consider the effect. He smiled and clapped his hands. 'All that glisters,' he said to no one. 'All that glisters. There it is.' He took off his leather coat and laid it on the pavement near the dog. He cradled the dog, taking care not to interfere with the wound, and slid the animal on to the coat. Then he lifted the dog in the coat, and began to walk with it held out flat in front of him, following the drops of Josh's blood on the pavement. He saw Josh's back disappearing towards the lights of Sloane Square. 'Oh Michael,' he trilled, 'wait for me. You really must look at this.'

Josh did not break stride. His footsteps echoed in the empty street. Francis called again. This time Josh hesitated and looked round. When he saw that Francis was carrying the dead dog, he began to run back towards him. 'Nooo,' he shouted. 'Are you mad? Put it down. Down or I'll fucking kill you.' Francis stopped and Josh stopped. There was a stand-off with Francis still holding the dog. 'I mean it,' said Josh. He raised his fists. 'I really mean it. *Gently*,' he warned as Francis made to toss the dog carcass on to the pavement.

Francis had only wanted to paint it, to capture it while the glitter was undulled. He had already painted carcasses of dead meat, sometimes in a state of crucifixion, and admitted to having a thing about butcher's shops. But here were innards that were only just dead, that retained the glistening, membranous freshness of life. Here was a challenge he fancied, even if it was three o'clock in the morning and he had been drinking since that first glass of hock in the French more than fifteen hours before. Norman Bowler said he had to get out of Soho before it destroyed him, as it destroyed many people he knew. But Bacon alone was immune to the devil's pact that Soho made you sign. Soho couldn't touch Francis. He became famous for his ability to work after drinking. Even epic sessions, which might lay low the other participants for several days, would see Bacon in his studio afterwards. He liked working with a hangover, he said, it made things crack and fizz in his head. What he intended now was to take the carcass back to Apollo Place and, there and then, before death had a chance to ruin things, paint and sketch the obscene brilliance of the dog's unzipped guts and organs. But you don't have to be Lucian's grandfather to understand why Josh was horrified by this idea. So, realizing he was about to come off worse – though even then thinking up another idea in its place – Francis backed down about the dog, and he and Josh lowered the carcass over the hedge where it fell among shrubs.

They continued walking towards the river, in silence at first while each digested the confrontation that had just taken place between them. Then Josh apologized for the strength of his reaction, and told the story of the dogs back in Liskeard. Francis replied by talking of his grandfather – not strictly his grandfather, as he corrected himself, but 'this frightful bastard who married my grandmother' – in Ireland whom he remembered torturing cats: he would toss them to the local hound pack and string them up around the house. 'I'm allergic to dogs,' finished Francis, 'but at present I do like to paint them. Oh well...'

The tide was coming up the river, bringing with it the fogs of the Essex marshes. The houseboats moored by Battersea Bridge lay invisible between water and mist. The bridge itself floated like a card trick on the mist. Number nine Apollo Place, which Henrietta Moraes was to inherit on Minton's suicide in 1957, is an impeccably bijou house with porthole windows on the landing and an artist's studio attached, at the end of a short mews behind Cheyne Walk. Minton is said to have made up his mind to buy it when he discovered that the wife of the friend who was selling it had killed herself there. Another attraction may have been the fact that J.M.W. Turner had painted in the studio next door. At Minton's invitation Francis lived and worked at number nine for a short time in the early 1950s though he and Johnny never got on terribly well, on account of their dislike of each other's work and of the latter's professional jealousy of Francis' rocketing fame. A famous Soho story has Bacon pouring a bottle of champagne over Minton's head (probably in the Colony Room) after some disagreement, and declaiming 'Champagne for my real friends, real pain for my sham friends'. It was one of his favourite phrases and always crops up in accounts of the era. Nevertheless, in Bacon's restless period Minton was gracious enough to offer him a temporary home, and Bacon wasn't too proud to accept.

Francis let them in and satisfied himself that Minton had not returned that night – he was probably still out trawling for the sailors who had done Josh in. Bacon showed Josh the bathroom so he could clean himself up and walked up the stairs to the studio attached to the side of the house.

Bacon had already colonized this studio, as if his soul were a skip he had voided there. If Deakin's studio was an analogue of creativity, Bacon's nightmarish vaults of detritus were paradigms of genius. Diarrhoeic blatterings of paint covered walls, doors and curtains. On shelves and chairs, paintbrushes sprouted from old jam pots like masts in a marina and fifteen pairs of spectacles suffered from dusty glaucoma. Pathways did exist between the pagodas of newspaper, the old Daz boxes, the tins of turpentine and linseed oil, the international magazines, the gilt-edged invitations and empty claret bottles, the broken easels, the odd mournful-looking tome of art theory or criticism; but, like a river pilot, you had to know the place in your bones, and only Francis could do that. Now, without turning on the lights, he stood in the midst of his domain as the first stirrings of day lightened the sky beyond the glass roof and, with one hand smoothing his hair back behind one ear and tugging at his collar, he contemplated a canvas propped on an easel in a corner.

It was a largish canvas, six-foot-six tall and four-foot-six wide, and it was largely blank, the natural, unpainted colour of parcel-paper-brown predominating. The only paint appeared slightly above the half-way point in a horizontal band: old-fashioned cars ran along what looked like a corniche, behind which was a single palm tree and a hesitant line of pale blue which the eye naturally saw as sea. Several times, Francis stepped up to and then backed away from this scarcely started painting, narrowing his eyes and cocking his head on one side like a – well, like a dog hearing an unfamiliar sound. I have seen the completed version of this painting – it is owned by the Tate Gallery and periodically on display there – and so I know how he finished it. Though the painting is a minor work of Bacon's there is something extremely unusual about it in terms of his canon: it offers a visual escape. Almost all of Bacon's subjects, be they popes or sides of meat, people he knew or hellish monsters, are locked into a proscribed world consisting variously of walls and ceilings, plinths, beds and even the suggestion of glass boxes, and rarely, if ever, doors. It is almost without exception a locked-in, indoors world featuring domestic but oddly solace-free touches such as bare lightbulbs, chairs, toilets, patterned carpets and striped mattresses. This is life and, for our brief spasm of consciousness between the void from which we spring and the void to which we return, there is no escaping the horror of it. Except that in the then unfinished painting propped on the easel in Apollo Place, the night that Josh came to stay, there is a way out. When things get too hairy in the foreground, as one knows they will, you can step into the back of the painting, cross the corniche and stand in the shade of that palm tree contemplating the ocean. You can even immerse yourself in that ocean. Is this the happiest painting that Bacon ever painted?

'Where do I go?' said Josh. He stood in the doorway to the studio, looking around in wonder at the clutter. His face was washed of blood, his nose was swollen and blue on the bridge.

Francis smiled. 'Where would you like to go? There, if you like.' He pointed at the blank space on the canvas.

'Where's that?' said Josh.

'Anywhere you like,' said Francis. 'Let's say Monte Carlo. You'll like it, I promise. I've never been happier than in Monte. The tables, the *impossible* men with big yachts and miracle cures. What do you think? I'm serious.'

Josh shrugged. 'What do I do?'

'I'll show you,' said Francis; and somehow, from the debris and chaos, he produced two cut-glass tumblers and a bottle of Martini.

JOHN MINTON AND ACTRESS NICOLETTE BERNARD (HULTON
GETTY)

Chapter 10

Francis Bacon, as I've said, rarely painted from life, from a model in the studio. He preferred to take inspiration from pictures in magazines or newspapers, or from commissioned photographs, of which John Deakin provided many, including portraits of Henrietta and Lucian Freud. Another favourite source was the extraordinary photographic studies by Eadweard Muybridge. In the 1880s, in California and later at the University of Pennsylvania in Philadelphia, Muybridge evolved a method of taking sequences of photographs a fraction of a second apart which for the first time captured the true nature of physical movement. Muybridge it was who established that horses did not run splay-legged, as in those weird old paintings of horse races, but in the asymmetrical fashion which we now take for granted. He also invented the zoopraxiscope, a forerunner of the movie camera which enabled his photographs to be projected in rapid succession, thus giving the impression of movement. Muybridge's ground-breaking work, which showed both humans and animals engaged in all sorts of activities, was first published in eleven volumes and called *Animal Locomotion; an electro-photographic investigation of consecutive phases of animal movements*. Artists and scientists such as John Ruskin, Auguste Rodin and Louis Pasteur were captivated by it. Half a century later, so was Bacon.

Muybridge was assisted and advised in his mammoth project by all sorts of academics and technicians, by pedants of perspective and sticklers for the systematic. Cameras with automatic trigger mechanisms and high-speed shutters took their stop-motion photographs from three different positions simultaneously; a grid painted on the background wall was intended as an aid to accurate draughtsmanship. Thus a sequence showing, say, 'Woman walking', would feature eighteen frames of a female figure engaged in this most humdrum of activities: six taken from the side; six taken simultaneously from the front and printed directly below; and six taken from the rear, also simultaneously, and printed below *them*. Taken together, the sequences present an exhaustive study of female perambulation. Eleven volumes filled with similarly meticulous and methodologically unimpeachable observations – a worthy but deadly dull body of work, surely? Not a bit of it. Not least because the woman who appears in 'Woman walking' is naked; she has hair down to the small of her back, smallish, pert breasts, a neat black triangle of pubic hair, and the ghost of a smile on her chubby face. In fact, every one of the hundreds of models used by Muybridge in his multi-volume opus is naked except, here and there, for those engaged in genital-threatening activities such as boxing or horse-riding (they wear jockstraps).

Not only that. The activities Muybridge and his team of advisors had their models demonstrate range from the predictable and useful 'Woman walking' to the bizarre and surreal: 'Legless boy climbing out of chair'; 'Chicken scared by a torpedo'. The effect of this ostensibly scientific undertaking is sometimes distasteful and often hilarious or erotic, as if, somewhere along the line, Muybridge had subverted the original idea and bamboozled his high-minded colleagues in the cause of something altogether more disturbing. The sequence entitled 'Toilet, stooping and throwing wrap around shoulders', for instance, is instantly and gratuitously sexual. It features a woman with long dark hair, naked except for shiny black pumps, bending to pick up a diaphanous wrap from the floor and then throwing it around her shoulders, pivoting as she does so. In the top row, taken from the side, her white body against the black background looks rather like a series of hieroglyphs; in the middle row, taken from the front, she faces the camera, squatting rudely as she picks up the wrap and then turning coyly away from the camera in the last frame as if suddenly realizing the lens is snooping at her. It is the final sequence which gives this study its erotic charge, for this is shot from the rear. Not only does the woman's bottom jut suggestively at the camera in the first frame but in the last she turns to the camera as if to flaunt her nakedness. Who were these happy and shameless Americans who spanked children, kicked hats, and let it all hang out for science and Crazy Man Muybridge?

Bacon sometimes made direct homage to Muybridge, as in a late composition entitled *After Muybridge – Study of the Human Figure in Motion – Woman Emptying a Bowl of Water – Paralytic Child on All Fours*. Most famously, however, Muybridge inspired Bacon's most overtly erotic painting. *Two Figures*, painted in the year he met Josh, is sometimes called *The Wrestlers* after Muybridge's sequence showing two naked wrestlers and entitled 'Wrestling: Graeco-Roman'. The painting, now owned by Lucian Freud and seldom exhibited, is also known as *Two Buggers* after the activity Bacon sought to depict, which wasn't wrestling. So shocking was this work considered to be that at an exhibition at the Hanover Gallery in 1953, it was hung upstairs in an obscure corner to prevent the police seeing it. That same year, Bacon produced another Muybridge-inspired painting; or rather part-Muybridge-inspired, for Muybridge does not provide the whole picture. For that, we must turn to Josh.

It was Josh's snarling, feral turn against the sailors in Meard Street which gave Bacon the idea to paint him. He had noticed Josh in the Gargoyle, of course. He had watched Josh's fragmented, repeated image in the mirrored wall as Henrietta had dragged him off to the Ladies. When Francis looked at a potential subject through the Gargoyle's mirrored wall, he was also looking at the ghost of the finished artwork. He had remarked Josh's compact body and blithe gait, how they could be made to work on canvas. Down among the cobbles of Meard Street, it was the animal in Josh that Francis sat up and noticed. Minus two teeth, Josh rose from the ground bloodied but fearless. His fists came up, as they had in a brothel in Auckland two years before, and moved in a blur in front of his chest, not making contact, but ticking over like an idling but powerful engine. It hadn't been a fair contest. He had been jumped on before he'd had time to deploy his boxing skills; but now he would show these two thugs how handy he was. 'Come ong theng,' he had said, but the fight had gone out of his assailants. Josh dropped his fists, but not before Francis had seen them moving, blurred with speed, and got what he wanted.

Now Bacon scrabbled impatiently among the layers of crap on the studio floor. Through the skylight, dawn had swelled, touching the nape of Bacon's neck and the corded backs of his hands, transforming the chaos with a sort of kindness. On a sofa in the corner, Josh lay asleep. One hand, outstretched, still held a tumbler with Martini in it. Noticing this, Bacon stepped over, removed the glass, drained it of drink before screwing out a space for it on the floor, and folded Josh's arm gently back across his chest. Then he resumed his low-level search. After a while he exclaimed, 'There it is!' and held aloft, for the unconscious Josh's inspection, a small sheaf of tatty leaves torn from a book of Muybridge studies.

The pages showed various animals in motion: horses

trotting, a pig shuffling, a gnu galloping (irregularly). Bacon riffled through these impatiently until he came to the dog. He threw the other pages back down among the detritus while he studied this page. It was entitled 'Kate Turning Around' and showed a spaniel being surprised by a sound or movement to her rear, her most vulnerable part. Kate's head and shoulders are whipping around, her eyes and ears alert. If one could narrow one's eyes to turn them into a zoopraxiscope, one would see a vortex of fur and flashing teeth, of glistening mouth and corrugated muzzle. One would see controlled aggression, and imagine the snap and snarl. Bacon held the page towards Josh. His eyes darted from Turning Kate to Sleeping Josh, and he nodded, stroking back his hair with his free hand.

The Routemaster wheezed north up Sloane Street. From the saloon deck, I looked right at the sunken gardens of Cadogan Place. Against these railings Bacon found the dead dog, and into the corner of these gardens he and Josh respectfully lowered the carcass, turning it into nutrients for the grubs and shrubs. I mused on how things are enriched in ways we dare not consider. The elderly woman in front, for instance, the woman whom I took to be Cecilia, was enriching me this very second – that soft nape, the gauzy, fly-away feel of her – though she would have no idea, would think her days of enriching men, as, briefly, she had enriched and humanized Josh nearly fifty years ago, were long gone.

Chugging along in the warm bus, the skin of it vibrating like a panting cat, Cecilia sitting upright and patient as a small girl. Knightsbridge, Hyde Park Corner, Piccadilly. Into the heart of things, the journey that Josh took. I knew, suddenly, where Cecilia was going. As we passed the Royal Academy, she stirred, began to gather, with the unhurried particularity of old age, her things about her. At a red light, she made her move, shuffled past me down the aisle without a glance. At Piccadilly Circus I waited until the last moment. The bus shook and seemed to exhale with relief as people got off. As the last one dropped and the driver found first gear, I jumped up and nipped off myself. I hung back by Tower Records as I located her in the pavement crowds. There she was, waiting to cross towards Burger King. This was the collar around Soho, the last of the bubblewrap. Tourists and Londoners streamed around Cecilia, all of them taller, stronger, faster. I kept losing her in the swell of walking wear and black leather, and madmen babbling on invisible mobiles. But then she would bob up again, hat floating happily on the tide. The press of people didn't feel so claustrophobic when I had a prey to keep in view, and besides, we were soon enough inside those bohemian ramparts. No, what bothered me more was that the past began, for the first time, to feel distant, to appear to me as the palest of ghosts. Josh, for instance, might have walked this way on the day he first met Farson, arrowing in towards his destiny. But there was no Josh at my side now, bouncing along in his greatcoat, smile of triumph on his face from having fooled the copper. There was just an old lady in front.

Sensibly, she avoided the raging currents of Shaftesbury Avenue by cutting up the backwater of Sherwood Street – beneath the Bridge of Sighs at the back of the Regent Palace Hotel, where homeless kids lie begging in blue sleeping bags – and right into Brewer Street. Thus we slipped into the square mile unnoticed, true *habitués*. Progress was painfully slow. As Cecilia worked her way east along the south side of Brewer Street, I crossed and re-crossed the street behind her, willing on the ghosts: past the locksmith's and the sushi bar, past the bottom of Great Pulteney Street, where the composer Haydn leant from his lodgings window one morning and remarked that the fog was so thick you could spread it on toast;

past the Everything for Lefthanders Shop and the Vintage Magazine Shop, past the art deco NCP car park, past Ann Summers, Swedish Strip and Adult Playthings, past the Raymond Revuebar, Madame Jo Jo's, Little Amsterdam and Trashy Lingerie, past the kind of £1 peepshow that turns into a £150 fleecing; past a girl with peroxide hair and blotchy cleavage whose invitation to step inside died on her lips when she saw me – meaning, I realized with a rush of gratitude, I did not look to her like a dickbrain from Doncaster. Past all these things and not a whiff of, say, Blake or Shelley, let alone dear old Josh. Cecilia was all I had left.

When she reached Wardour Street, and paused on the kerb as the despatch riders burnt past, I thought for a moment that once she had crossed she would turn left and head for Meard Street. A fantasy flickered in my head: that at the far end of Meard Street she would turn through the heavy porch of number sixty-nine and disappear through the studded door beyond; I would follow her there, summon back the lift she had just taken to the top and, in that rickety elevator with its wooden panelling and concertinaed grille of a door, defy time by rising back through the decades. Well, Cecilia doused that one by turning not left but right on the far side of Wardour Street, and then first left into Old Compton Street. Here I stopped by a shop window displaying gay bondage gear in order to let Cecilia get ahead. And as I waited there, not-quite-looking at the dog collars and batwing waistcoats, a figure shambled past that looked familiar. It was Norman Balon, landlord of the Coach and Horses in Greek Street, though how I recognized him I hardly knew. Norman was the miserable-fucker publican of Jeffrey Bernard's 'Low Life' column in the *Spectator*, who billed himself as the rudest landlord in London. He had a face like Walter Matthau's and a genuinely unpleasant manner. Now here he was trudging along Old Compton Street, stooped and mordantly scowling, with a thin green plastic bag swinging at his side. I supposed I had been in the Coach over the years and got to know what Norman looked like, though it was a shock to see and recognize him so unhesitatingly as he had, for me, assumed the profile of a fictional character by this time. As he overtook Cecilia he flapped a hand in an offhand wave, to which she responded with the merest tilt of her hat.

When, at the junction with Dean Street, Cecilia crossed to the south side of Old Compton Street, there was suddenly no doubt where she was going. The French now came into view: the blue window canopies advertising Lanson champagne, the tricolours and union jacks and fleurs-de-lis. As Cecilia stepped in one door, the southerly, I entered by the other. Cecilia was greeted by a general murmur of approbation, punctuated by the odd 'Darling!' and 'How nice to see you', to which she returned a couple of vague 'Darling!'s herself, to no one in particular. A respectful space opened around her. Without receiving instruction the barman got busy on her drink while she inched herself on to a bar stool, placed the pale-blue packet of cigarettes before her on the bar top and removed her hat. It was this last action which gave the game away. As she took off the hat, unnaturally black hair fell about her face which now, at last, was revealed to me; red lips in an oval face that was ravaged but still with beauty. Though I couldn't see her neck for the scarf tied there, there was no doubt that Cecilia was dewlap-lady! She took the bloody Mary, drank and beckoned to the barman, who wordlessly, placed the Lea & Perrins bottle in front of her. 'He can't believe how much sauce I like,' she announced, fumbling with her cigarette packet. 'Can't fucking believe it! Gets him every time. Ha!'

'It won't be the fags that kill you,' replied the barman, 'that's for sure. Are you well, anyway?'

Needless to say, I witnessed all this with open-mouthed fascination from the other end of the bar. When the barman moved down to serve me he had to click his fingers in front of my face to gain my attention. When he realized I had been watching Cecilia he said something about her being a character, and I agreed that she was. I knew now that I must talk to her, that it was ridiculous that I had not done so already. But first some Dutch courage. I ordered a half of Guinness and my usual glass of white to keep it company; finished the wine before I had drunk a third of the Guinness and ordered another; finished the Guinness before I had drunk more than a half of the second glass of wine and ordered another Guinness; had another glass of Macon Villages for the hell of it. And it was while I was drinking and glancing every so often at Cecilia, and trying to work out what my opening gambit would be, and worrying about whether I would be overheard, as conversation in the French tended to be communal property; it was while such thoughts were flicking through my mind like a gnu through Muybridge's zoopraxiscope, that I had the idea of buying Cecilia flowers and presenting them to her at the bar. It would be an icebreaker as well as an appropriate gesture. So I drained the last of my wine and, checking one last time that Cecilia was still safely installed at the bar, made my way, swaying somewhat, to Berwick Street to buy flowers. I had another brainwave on the way: I would buy two bouquets, one for Cecilia and another for Louise, whom, I was reminding myself periodically and excitedly, I was due to meet later. And this is what I did. But when I returned to the French, laden with blooms and resolved in my drunken state to approach Cecilia and explain myself, she had gone. Though her hat and cigarettes had vanished from the bar top, I persuaded myself for some minutes that she had merely gone to the lavatory. But when another regular came in and occupied the stool she had sat on, I had to confront the truth: I had missed her. Ordering another glass of wine from behind the mobile floristry I had saddled myself with, I asked the barman casually what had happened to the 'character' who'd been sat at the bar. Did he happen to know where she'd gone? The barman's mood darkened when I asked this. 'Who wants to know?' he said.

I didn't know what to say.

Josh did not keep his appointment with the casting director of *Sea Devils*, on account of having two teeth missing and his nose plastered half way across his face. If the fight hadn't happened and he had bowled up at the Dorchester, hair Vaselined and chin piratically stubbled, things might have been different; as they might have been had he realized who David Archer was when Archer propositioned him during their afternoon drinking session in the Gargoyle. Maybe, if Josh had accepted the invitation of the bespectacled bookseller and publisher to return to his flat in Bayswater and recite some of his poems, he would have become the published poet he always fancied being. Granted, Josh's poems, from what people have seen of them, were hardly exceptional; but a little bit of novel naivety ('The Sailor Poet') finessed with verbs and punctuation could have gone a long way. But Josh did not become a poet or an actor in the summer of 1953. He became the thing he was when he died. Thanks to Bacon, he became a painter and decorator.

Bacon advised him to lie low for a while, to wait for tempers to settle down before returning to Soho. For now, Bacon told him, there was plenty to occupy Josh at Apollo Place without the need to venture into town. While living at Cromwell Place, South Kensington, in the immediate post-war years, Bacon had hosted many illegal gambling evenings inspired by his recent happy times in the casino at Monte Carlo. Amid the rubble outside, and the chintz and fag ash within, and as if people hadn't had enough risk and terror to last several lifetimes, high rollers and desperate mugs had gratified their addictions to these very opiates at the roulette wheel and the baize-topped table. Unlicensed gambling on private premises, especially involving the high sums that some of Bacon's friends won and lost, carried heavy penalties if found out. For this reason, and in counterpoint to his recklessness at the tables, Bacon was scrupulously cautious about security. When gambling was in progress he would employ three or four lookouts to hang around outside the house and along the street. As cover, he would dress them in overalls and give them paint-brushes and buckets of paint. At Apollo Place, Bacon consulted Johnny Minton who agreed that he could resume his gaming evenings, albeit on a more modest and occasional basis. Johnny, who loved sailors, was happy for Josh to stick around. Bacon told Minton he would kit Josh out in overalls and pay him to be a lookout when gambling was going on. 'He might even paint your house while he's about it,' said Bacon.

Apollo Place is a short cul-de-sac. Number nine is at the end and its front door and porthole-shaped landing window face back up this dead-end towards the cross street, Riley Street, which in turn abuts Cheyne Walk and the Thames Embankment just a few yards to the south-east. Apollo Place was so short a street that trouble could be round the corner in either direction from Riley Street before Josh would have time to warn the gamblers within. And it wasn't as if number nine Apollo Place was unknown to the police, as the traffic of Minton's reprobate friends through its doors had several times resulted in visits from the constabulary. To have a decent view of the approaches, Josh realized, he would need to get high. 'The paintbrush is fine,' he said to Bacon, 'but I need a ladder.' A ladder was found in the back garden, an old wooden ladder with some rungs missing and others dangerously weak-ened. Bacon and Minton watched Josh carry it through the house from back to front, so lost in their admiration for his patient manner in reconciling angle of wall and length of ladder, not to mention his pursed lips, and the beads of sweat between the eyes, that they forgot to help him. 'I must paint him,' thought Minton. He and Bacon followed Josh outside, looking forward to the next performance: seeing him climb. Josh grinned when he felt their eyes on his back. 'Just watch me,' he said.

He started slowly, testing each rung, and it was as well he did as several snapped. He reached the lip of the mansard roof and levered himself up on to the gentle upper slope, where he sat and tried out his field of vision: river and bridge to the right, enough of Riley Street dead ahead for him to give a couple of minutes' warning at least. He looked down on the upturned faces of Bacon and Minton and gave them the thumbs up. They waved and were about to go inside when he stopped them. 'Wait,' he shouted down. 'Watch this.' And he did his Button Boy trick, shinning up the chimney stack, standing on the top and giving a salute which earned a round of applause from below.

'I must paint him.' Minton said it out loud this time, and Bacon smiled and said nothing. Up on the roof, on the tiled slopes and the felt-and-tar horizontals, among the nests of skylights, the odd dormer window and the huge pitched glass roof of the adjacent studio, Josh spent many late summer evenings tiptoeing and free, as the skies turned green over the river. He did paint the house, as Johnny – generous as ever and half in love – promised him extra money for doing it. Preparing and painting the window frames, a time-consuming job, enabled him to look in through the windows, as a child peers into a doll's house, and see a hundred lives going on beyond. Minton no longer operated quite the open house policy he had at previous of his London addresses. In the summer of 1953, in the wake of the defections of Burgess and MacLean, the Home Office and Scotland Yard had announced a crackdown on 'male vice' and 'filth spots' – a half-baked attempt to minimize the threat to establishment people of blackmail for homosexual activities. Minton was very open about his gayness. He had even gone public, in print, a brave thing to do when to be actively gay was still a criminal offence punishable by imprisonment. In 1950 he had had a letter published in the *Listener* pointing out 'The enormous contribution made throughout history – particularly in the arts – to society by homosexuals' and asking for 'a saner and more comprehensive attitude towards the homosexual in society'. Nevertheless, the new climate of intolerance he sensed in 1953 made him nervous. He apparently destroyed a number of erotic drawings he had done, and decided to keep the front door of Apollo Place firmly shut.

The traffic of young men continued however. As he worked on the roof, Josh heard them before he saw them tripping up Apollo Place; Johnny's Circus of art students in floppy collars and capes braying about Pablo Picasso and conical bras, or musclebound hunks with bottles weighing down the pockets of their donkey jackets. Sometimes Josh would break off from his painting to study them; track them as far as the front door, then turn round and watch them, through the various skylights and windows, disperse through the rooms of the house. In silence, while paint dripped on to Josh's boots from his motionless brush, they broke open bottles, dropped glasses, embraced, laughed, jitterbugged to the gramophone. No one danced more fiercely than Johnny nor cried more rackingly when he was on his own. Johnny loved Keith and Keith loved Johnny, but Keith disapproved of his promiscuity and found someone steady; Ricky loved Johnny but preferred sleeping with girls; Ricky hated art but liked money and Johnny loved Ricky and hated himself. Josh didn't feel excluded by this mad dance. He came down off the roof every so often to brew a tea and it must have been at this time that he first properly met Norman Bowler. Somebody would think they recognized him from, say, the Gargoyle, and offer him a bottle or a glass but he generally declined, evincing even then a surprising work ethic, a duty to detail, which would make him in later life a very good painter and decorator. Besides, Minton's scene at Apollo Place was like Soho in miniature and he had had enough of Soho for now.

One thing these old Sohoites repeated to me was that too many people made the mistake of not having any home life. Some, like Josh, literally did not have a home to go to and had to take whatever they could blag. Josh did very well in this respect. The occasions on which he ended up on a park bench, as he had in his early Soho days, were few compared to the decent beds and solace he sniffed out and held on to. Others had perfectly good homes but forgot to go there; yet others, like John Minton, took Soho back to their homes. And after a while they forgot who they were beyond the characters they played with a glass in their hand. It became impossible to see these barflies as owners of front-door keys and putter-outers of dustbins. The Minton of Lucian Freud's heart-breaking 1952 painting *Portrait of John Minton* is fragile as a dandelion clock and you imagine him wafting away to nothing at closing time, only to appear miraculously reconstituted the next morning on the dot of eleven-thirty or noon, depending which side of Oxford Street he had a mind to drink on.

At Apollo Place, Josh enjoyed again the kind of brief domestic contentment he had had with Cecilia in her parents' Hampstead house. He managed this by steering clear of Minton and his circle and sticking with Francis and his gambling cronies. Come the evening Johnny's Circus flew to town, flitting off like butterflies through the dusk. Francis, who had been working in the studio all day, would then invite Josh down for a drink, and Josh would ask to see the portrait of himself that Francis was working on, and Francis would graciously refuse to show him, and they would have another drink instead. Then limousines with running boards would slide up to the riverside, and Bacon's gambling friends, overcoated and deliberate, more moth than butterfly, would begin to arrive. Here were art dealers and aeroplane designers, con men and distracted professorial types, a lesbian heiress and her bodyguard, an ex-jockey with a limp – an improbable ragbag who thrilled to the music of chance. Riding a streak of luck, Bacon once won £1,600 in an evening at the casino in Monte Carlo. In those hours when his numbers came up over and over again, he felt like the author of his own life; he saw the balls landing before they landed, he hallucinated his own omnipotence. Bacon's paintings eschewed narrative; life was too random to be explained by stories. Yet stories are what keep you sane and even Francis – who generally didn't believe in them – needed stories. Well, he believed in them at the roulette wheel.

Josh was the coat-taker and drink-fixer. I can imagine him taking to this role. Though sometimes violent and unpredictable when drunk, Josh could have a lovely manner to him when sober – solicitous and discreet. The first time I met him, down at Greensands when I was on leave from boarding school where individual privacy was considered decadent, I remember he instantly charmed and relaxed me with a smile of still-powerful wattage. Then he put a glass of beer in my hand and pushed his pouch of tobacco across the table at me: 'Do you? Help yourself.'

'Oh Josh,' said Jean, but I could tell she was proud of him.

In the Apollo Place casino Josh took the coats and fixed the Martinis, and when the wheels began to spin and the balls to clack he went back up on to the roof to keep guard, watching the sun paint the river and gazing down, through the glass roof of the studio, on to the canvas which held his unfinished likeness. He had been puzzled that Francis did not want him to sit for the portrait, as Minton had had him do.

Bacon had explained that he rarely worked from life, that he preferred working from photographs or even just mental images. This was all very well, thought Josh, when the subject was busy, or lived in an inconvenient place, but when Josh was on the premises already, it seemed a shame that Francis didn't take advantage of that fact. Privately, he was worried that the finished painting would not be as faithful a portrait of him as if Bacon had painted him from life. It seemed like a missed opportunity which might result in a likeness as obscure as the Deakin photograph, in which you could hardly see him for shadow. He had tried to get a view of the canvas through the roof to see how it was progressing – all he could make out clearly was the background he had seen when he first came to Apollo Place, of the corniche and palm tree. Below that, there was definitely paint on the canvas where previously there had been none, but he could not make out precisely what it was.

Bacon was deliberately obfuscatory when it came to his methods of working. He always claimed that it was a hit-and-miss affair; that he never drew out his compositions on the canvas beforehand, and that often he would arrive at a figure or composition by happy accident; that the painting he thought he intended would turn into something entirely different in front of his eyes as he worked with the paint on the canvas. There's no doubt a large element of deliberate myth-making to this, for Bacon was much more in control of his work than he liked to let on. On the other hand, this idea of the happy accident perhaps did apply to his portrait of Josh, or rather the portrait that Josh inspired. When he worked, Bacon was careful not to let anyone into the studio and Josh was careful not to barge in. But while Josh was up on the roof and painting the house, he couldn't help seeing Francis working below, through the glass roof. As he sometimes paused in his painting-and-decorating to spy on Johnny's Circus, so he would take advantage of his view point to watch Bacon in the process of painting. It looked to Josh less like painting, as he imagined it, than violent disagreement, as if Bacon was conducting a no-holds-barred argument with the canvas. He stepped up to it, brush in hand, and taunted it with flashing arabesques, he stabbed it in the midriff, he rubbed his stubbled chin against its cheek, and in between such sallies he withdrew to gauge their effect, head cocked on one shoulder as he took in the damage. Sometimes the violence would become literal. Several times, through the glass roof, Josh had seen Bacon take a razor blade or a knife to a canvas and slash it to shreds. In fact Bacon had warned that his portrait of Josh might be destroyed before it was completed, and Josh had endured an anxious few days before Bacon assured him it was in fact going reasonably well and almost certainly would see the light of day.

The possibility that he might never have seen the painting made the idea of it all the more precious to Josh. He became more insistent in his requests to see it, and Francis became irritated by that insistence. In the evenings before the gamblers arrived, when Francis was in the studio changing into one of his smart suits, Josh would appear unexpectedly in the doorway, hoping for a glimpse of the painting. And there it would be, but always draped with a sheet, always covered up – more maddening for Josh, one supposes, than not seeing it at all. Josh understood that he was not welcome in the studio while Francis worked. But once he was summoned off the roof for his early evening drink, he saw nothing wrong in sidling in and casting a startled eye over the baboons and open-mouthed heads and offal on mattresses. Francis had developed a certain dependency on Josh at this time. It was often Josh who got him out of bed in the morning, holding the pills he needed to get him started while Francis popped them one by one; making him tea he never drank; asking favours of Minton on Bacon's behalf. While Bacon accepted this kind of attention as his due, Josh perhaps made the mistake of assuming he was beginning to occupy a place of some importance in Bacon's life.

One evening Francis was in a state of evident excitement. His work had gone well that day and he was looking forward to welcoming an important guest, a Parisian gallery owner, to the Apollo Place casino. 'Did you bring back my suit from the dry cleaner?' he asked as Josh mooched among the canvases, glancing every so often at the one draped with a sheet. 'You did remember?' he said, his voice hitting a note of rising anger and panic when Josh did not immediately reply.

'What?' said Josh. 'Oh yes.'

'Well where is it?'

'Hanging in the hall,' said Josh.

'Well bring it in, bring it in,' said Bacon; and then, when Josh continued to skulk, hands in pockets, around the studio: 'What's the matter with you? I'll do it myself.'

Bacon strode with a sigh from the studio and returned with the freshly cleaned suit. He tossed the suit on a trestle table covered in paint pots, smears and dollops of wet paint and dirty rags, and walked to the back of the studio where he rummaged in a cupboard, shouting back over his shoulder, 'Where's my pancake and boot polish? It's *too* bad, it really is.'

Josh looked at the suit lying among the paint and muck on the table. He picked up the suit and hung it out of the way, on a high hook on the wall. Francis sat at the back in front of a small mirror. He had found what he wanted. He applied the foundation to his face with swift, expert strokes. He opened the tins of boot polish and examined them, muttering to himself. 'What shall I be tonight? Auburn? *Marron? Marron, Je pense.*' He took a cloth and smeared polish from the tins – dark tan, mid tan, cherry – onto the back of one hand where he mixed it with a shoe brush. He then brushed his hair with the shoe brush, spreading the polish evenly from Tony Curtis quiff to nape. He studied the effect in the mirror for some time, bobbing his head, holding a hand mirror behind his head. '*Voilà*,' he said eventually. '*Ça va*, Francis.'

It had been a very self-contained and unselfconscious performance, as if Francis were alone. Josh was smoking a cigarette, waiting for Bacon to acknowledge him again. Now Bacon walked towards him, glanced at the trestle table where he had laid the suit and stopped with a show of astonishment. He frowned and looked around. He saw the suit hanging up and, brushing past Josh as if he wasn't there, took down the suit from its wall hook and flung it back down among the crap on the table. Then he walked out of the studio.

As if reading Josh's shattered mind, Bacon reappeared a few seconds later in the doorway. 'Don't look at the painting,' he said. 'Just don't. Do you understand? You're like Jesus for Christ's sake, creeping around. What happened to you?'

Rather like John Minton, Bacon liked his friends either clever or pretty, but not both. Josh was the dumb, pretty type, the angelic street urchin, and it wouldn't do for him to be getting too domesticated or questioning. Josh, who couldn't help being pretty, would have loved to have been thought clever by Francis; by any of them, but especially by Francis. It was, he said, the story of his life. 'I don't care,' replied Josh. He strode towards the canvas with the sheet on it.

Bacon called out: 'Let me tell you! You're not the person I painted.'

Josh pulled the sheet from the canvas and stared at what it revealed. Seconds passed as he took in what Francis had painted. Half way up was the familiar corniche, with cars and palm tree. The bottom half of the picture was occupied by a space suggestive of a public park. A hexagon of virgin canvas, looking rather like raked gravel, was framed by what you might take to be a lawn, except the 'grass' was painted pillarbox-red. Within the hexagon of 'gravel' was a green oval that could have been a flower bed or disc of grass. On it was a figure. Its shoulders were blurred, caught in the act of turning. Its mouth was open, revealing a viscera-red tongue. It blazed animal anger and aggression. 'It's a fucking dog,' said Josh eventually.

LIMEHOUSE NIGHTS: FARSON (2nd LEFT), DEAKIN (3rd LEFT) AND BACON (RIGHT) WITH DOCKERS (ESTATE OF DANIEL FARSON)

Chapter 11

I took a cab to the Grapes in the end, being a bit the worse for wear. I hadn't intended to get drunk before meeting Louise. I had rather thought we might get pleasantly drunk together while I told her about Henrietta Moraes and Miss Abbey Potterson and the whole gallimaufry of coincidence and fate which had brought us to this point. I made a mental note to slow down on the drinking. We had arranged to meet at seven but it was only five-thirty when I arrived and I was already half gone. I made do with a half of bitter and had a mooch around the near-empty bar, taking in the Dickensian caricatures and marine charts, the old blurred photograph of cockney girls dancing to a street organ, the prints showing the back of the inn from the water, the wooden verandah and weatherboarding jutting picturesquely, dropsically bulging, indeed, above the tide.

In one of the prints, a gent in a stovepipe hat stood on the verandah waving to a lighterman in his flat-bottomed boat below. I opened the double doors at the back and stepped onto that verandah. I wasn't alone. A couple in office clothes were sharing an early evening bottle of wine and motoring through the Silk Cuts. The woman glanced up and dropped her voice when she saw me. Dragging deeply on her cigarette she muttered, 'So I said, "Just get outta my *fuck*ing hair." Know what I mean?' The river was up: wide and silvered. A tug beat downriver against the tide, pulling two barges of yellow containers. It was a non-committal, very English sort of day, grey and dampish though the rain had held off. I settled down, at the far end of the balcony from the couple, with my notes and books on Soho so I could get my stories word perfect for Louise.

You can get tongue-tied when you meet people for the first time and I wanted things to go smoothly. I had with me a couple of photographs of Henrietta; that is to say, Henrietta in the early 1950s. One showed her naked on a bed; one of the shots Deakin took for Bacon and later flogged to sailors in the French. I liked that story. I should tell Louise that one first, just to get the ball rolling. Then, having gauged the mood, I might or might not repeat the suggestion that Louise resembled Henrietta – not, I would hasten to add, that I would presume to know what she looked like naked: I would emphasize that I meant in a strictly facial sense. And so I boned up on Soho and rehearsed the likely course and pitfalls of our conversation. It was while idly leafing through one of my books on the era – one of the myriad accounts in which Josh is not given his due – that I made another odd discovery. The building a few doors down from the Grapes, now a wine bar called Booty's, was once Daniel Farson's house; and by coincidence, Francis Bacon had briefly lived in Narrow Street a decade later, conceivably (it wasn't clear) in the house Farson had owned. Here was a photograph of Bacon taken on Farson's balcony at Narrow Street in the early 1960s. I held up the book to the river light. Bacon is in mid conversational flow, mouth open, hands weighing air for emphasis, or perhaps to indicate *comme ci, comme ça*. The Grapes was at number seventy-six Narrow Street, Booty's eight doors to the east at number ninety-two. The picture would have been taken just over there, beyond where the couple were sitting. Behind them, at right angles to the back wall of the pub, was a wooden screen which prevented customers from prying into the backs of adjacent houses. I stood on my chair to see if I could see over or round the screen, but it wasn't possible. The couple stopped talking and stared for several seconds in my direction. I sat back down and resumed my reading.

Bacon moved to Narrow Street in 1970, a long time after he knew Josh. 'I have just bought the house I shall be murdered in,' he is reputed to have said. Moving east after a lifetime living in Chelsea and Kensington was a romantic and, in the end, impractical change. By making the move he had wished to affirm his preference for the East End, in all its imagined horny-handed simplicity, over the world of frauds and hangers-on up West. But things didn't work out, no doubt partly because Bacon was much more complex than the self-myths he created and often ended up half-believing: there was East and West in Francis, even if he didn't always like to admit it. In any case, there was a specific reason for his decision to get rid of the Narrow Street house: the light. Even on a relatively dull day like today, it hurt the eyes. I glanced up at the roiling water moving like a field of light, and the blinding skies above the Canary Wharf complex to the east. Clouds scudded behind the calligraphy of cranes; compressors chugged and piledrivers thumped through the marshy mattress that was the Isle of Dogs. Like a homuncule, the future stirred and blinked, while around it the light shimmered and feinted. The play of sun on water, the constant tidal flux, produced a flickering light that Bacon said he found impossible to paint in. But it wasn't so much, one suspects, that this riverine light wasn't sufficiently predictable as that there was just too much of it. He didn't actually need light in the way that a conventional, figurative studio painter does. His way of working was to empty the airless and dark cupboards of his mind and he didn't want too much light shining in there while he did so.

I was tempted to nip down to Booty's wine bar for a quick

look but the old anxiety, that Louise might turn up at the Grapes then leave when she saw I wasn't there, reasserted itself. Perhaps, if things went well, I would suggest to Louise that we went to Booty's together. In the meantime, I ordered another half and asked the barmaid about *Our Mutual Friend*. She directed me to the back of the bar meals menu where it was written: 'Many London pubs claim a history but few can boast the literary connections of the Grapes ...' After a description of the Six Jolly Fellowship Porters, the menu concluded: 'It is, as Dickens described it, an experience to "soften the human breast".' The barmaid then admitted that the Six Jolly Fellowship Porters might have been based on any, or all, of a number of pubs in the area in Dickens' time. But it was true, she said, that the back of the Grapes was like in the book. It — what was the word?

'Bulges,' I said.

'That's it,' she said. 'Bulges, in a sort of lopsided way, over the Thames. And Dickens is supposed to have stayed here. The scary thing is, he's supposed to have stayed in my bedroom.'

'Have you seen him?' I asked.

'No,' she said. 'But the dog,' she pointed down at a moth-eaten Alsatian asleep on a beanbag, 'goes mental at the wall sometimes, for no apparent reason.'

I spent the half-hour before Louise arrived wondering if I would recognize her. While the bar had been relatively empty I had reckoned it would be obvious when she came in. I imagined her looking round nervously and me hailing her, putting her at her ease. But now the Grapes was filling up with office workers from Canary Wharf, time travellers across two centuries, and every other woman that came through the door peered around myopically before finding her friends. I realized I hardly remembered what she looked like. I had only seen her for a few seconds in the Canary Wharf office of my editor and since then she had become so conflated in my mind's eye with Henrietta Moraes that I had no distinct sense of her at all. Every time the door swung open and a figure came in – generally black-clad and clutching lighter and cigarette packet – I expected Henrietta's breasts and nose and sardonic mouth.

But then Louise did come in, and I recognized her straight away. She *was* Henrietta.

Josh wasn't alone in being dismayed by Bacon's portrayal of him. In 1960 Bacon broke with his usual practice by having Cecil Beaton sit for him in his studio. Beaton wrote that the first, unfinished portrait to come out of these sittings made him look like a 'monster cripple' with no head and four legs. Perhaps vanity got the better of him for he asked Bacon to have another go. This time, recalled Beaton, Bacon made him look like a senile businessman with elephantiasis. Josh, you may think, got off lightly.

Study of a Dog is one of three paintings of dogs that Bacon did at this time. The background – the sea and palm tree and cars moving along a corniche – Bacon took from an old postcard of Monte Carlo, where he had lived and gambled in the 1940s. The red hexagon surrounding the central figure is typical of the delimiting and claustrophobic frames he slung around his subjects. The physical form of the turning, snarling dog is taken from Muybridge. The spirit of the beast is taken from Josh. Bacon began to explain this to Josh, and then gave up. He always said that if you could explain a painting in words, what was the point in having painted it? Bacon's former lover, Eric Hall, bought *Study of a Dog* for £275 and immediately bequeathed it to the Tate Gallery, where it remains. Josh drifted away from Francis after the episode with the painting. There is no evidence that they fell out badly over it. No doubt, when he had thought about it, Josh didn't feel so bad about being portrayed as a dog for, of course, he loved dogs. But he didn't want to be forever thought of as feral. It was all very well for people like Francis or Dan Farson to idealize types like him; they thought the street was somehow noble and picturesque, but they had never had to live there. Josh drifted away from Francis because he knew he could only ever be a dog in the great painter's taxonomy. It was, at least partly, the same motive that drew him away from Farson, which shows, in one sense, what little headway he had made during his summer in Soho.

It was autumn now and Josh was back in Soho. Thinking to make a fresh start, he kept to the fringes, north of Oxford Street, in and around Charlotte Street, strictly known as Fitzrovia. He said he got drunk a few times with Dylan Thomas. Josh recalled an occasion – which sounds suspiciously apocryphal, not least because Thomas died in early November of that year – when they were in the Fitzroy Tavern and Caitlin Thomas rang in a fury from South Wales. 'Tell Dylan to get on a train this minute or he's dead.' Dylan was duly despatched by taxi to Paddington, and Josh continued drinking. An hour later, the door burst open and in spilled Dylan, to general consternation. After ordering a drink he explained that his Swansea train had stopped at Reading and, seeing a London train on the opposite platform he had decided to catch it. Josh had laughed, telling this story, whilst admitting it was a generally difficult time in which he was drinking far too much and not looking after himself. He was also losing his touch when it came to picking up women, no doubt on account of his increasingly distressed state. There was one very bad night when freezing fog came down and Josh had not managed to secure a bed for the night. Not being a seasoned street sleeper, he did not know where the hot grates were, ventilating printing presses or hotel heating systems, and spent all night fumbling round the fog-bound West End to stop himself freezing to death, just as De Quincey and Ann had done a hundred and fifty years before. It was at this time that he first met Hetta Empson and, briefly, moved in with her, though the bulk of the twelve years he spent with her is beyond the scope of this account.

William Empson had just been appointed Professor of English at Sheffield University after the couple had spent several years in China. While William worked in Sheffield Hetta remained in London, becoming, in the phrase of *The Times* obituary, 'the cynosure of a large circle', cultivating a salon scene in their Hampstead house which I have always assumed Josh tried to emulate, in a modest way, down in Greensands. Hetta picked Josh up in a bar in Soho or Fitzrovia. She was seventeen years older than him, almost forty. She had campaigned on behalf of black people in her native South Africa, driven a London ambulance during the Blitz, and harboured Communist students in Beijing during the Chinese civil war. She generally got what she wanted, and she wanted Josh. He got falling-down drunk with Hetta and they went to bed, though it would be several more months before Hetta regularized the arrangement by offering Josh an attic room in their house. He discovered the pubs of Hampstead, where he met Frank, then an office equipment salesman. He seemed to have set himself up for the winter. And then he made the mistake of going back to Soho.

He had money, courtesy of Hetta, and he wore a set of William's clothes, with absent-minded frays and darns, that made him feel serious-minded. He meant to impress people, one supposes. Francis cold-shouldered him in the French (and was the figure slipping out shortly after he came in Daniel Farson, with vengeance in his heart? Thinking about it afterwards, Josh suspected so). Hoping for better luck in the Gargoyle, he walked up to Meard Street and hung around outside the entrance of the club waiting for a familiar face who would sign him in. He had been there scarcely five minutes when he saw the policeman turn into the cobbled street from Dean Street. He thought nothing of it until he became aware that the copper's heavy footfalls had stopped. In that moment he realized what was happening, but managed to keep his cool. 'Michael Avery?' said the policeman. 'Ordinary Seaman Michael Avery? I'm arresting you—.'

Josh tried the old trick. 'Avery?' he said incredulously. He spread his arms and shrugged.

'I'm arresting you . . .' continued the policeman. He fumbled in his pocket and as he did so Josh belted him in the face, turned, and ran towards Wardour Street. As he ran, slithering across the cobbles, whoops of laughter escaped from his throat. He saw the square of light at the end of Meard Street that meant freedom, just as it had when he had fled from Farson. In his imagination he was already finessing the incident into a story to tell Hetta and Frank. He would turn right when he reached the safety of Wardour Street. To be on the safe side, he would continue running up to and across Oxford Street, then cut right to Tottenham Court Road where he could catch a bus to Hampstead. He would be knocking back wine in Hetta's kitchen within half an hour. He would be speculating darkly on who had given the tip-off; he would be laughing his head off, and vowing not to return to Soho for a long time.

Then a dark shape was blocking the square of light. It was a policeman in a cape. Josh tried to sidestep him but the copper moved the same way and held him fast, manoeuvring Josh into a head lock. As he struggled, Josh heard footsteps running up behind him. He was kicked repeatedly in the arse and in the thighs. His head was yanked up into orange light and he took blows to the face until he lost consciousness.

It was Henrietta; big-boned, broad shouldered, big-breasted. When she bent over me and spoke my name – with a question mark at the end, not entirely sure she'd got the right person – I felt she could have crushed me like an insect with the weight of her presence. Bacon made an exception with Henrietta when he painted her. He used the pornographic Deakin photographs to work from, but he also wanted her in the studio, naked, while he worked, so this electric presence of hers would fill up the room as it now filled up the bar of the Grapes. Would she see me sweating, detect the tremor in my voice? I could scarcely believe we were finally here together.

'I'll get them,' she said in that imperious, posh voice, as I arose on trembling legs to go to the bar. 'What'll you have?'

I had a joke half-prepared for this moment. 'Ask them,' I said, 'if they serve Dog's Nose.' Louise frowned. 'Just ask them.' I smiled and raised my eyebrows. She deposited her black briefcase on the chair next to me and went to the bar. I studied her from behind. Head-to-toe in black, topped with black hair, artfully ruffled. Heartbreaking concavity of lower back; tantalizing glimpse of neck and upper shoulders as she leant forward to attract the barmaid's attention.

She turned and shrugged. 'They haven't heard of Dog's Nose,' she said. Cheekbones catching the light from the old gas lamps above the bar. 'Come to that,' she muttered – half to herself, though I managed to catch it – 'neither have I.'

Good game, I thought. 'Fine,' I said. 'Make it a pint of bitter and a straight gin.' Disappointingly, Louise was drinking mineral water. I drank an inch off the top of my pint and plopped the gin in. 'Cheers,' I said, clinking her glass with mine. 'You really don't know what this is? This is a Dog's Nose. Bitter and gin. It's what they drank in the Gargoyle, remember?'

'I have no idea what you're talking about,' she said.

'You don't know the Gargoyle? Oh come on! What about the Colony Room? Muriel?' I gestured round the bar. 'Abbey Potterson?'

'Look . . .' she began.

I drank half of the Dog's Nose straight off. 'It doesn't matter,' I said. I felt sure I could deal with this if I just relaxed a little. If we both relaxed. Why wouldn't she have a proper drink? 'We've got plenty of time. Are you sure you won't have something alcoholic?'

'No, really,' she said. She looked at her watch. 'Did you manage to find it all right? This is a backwater these days. People don't realize such places still exist.'

'I caught a cab. I bought you some flowers.' I looked around in bafflement. 'But I think I must have left them in the cab.' We both smiled wanly, and it was then that I noticed the beads of sweat on her upper lip. Louise was nervous too. This was comforting. I raised my glass, said 'Cheers' again, and drank the rest of it off. I needed the courage that drink brings. I shook my head, making that funny sound you make when you wobble slack cheeks. 'I'll have another one of those,' I said.

'Please do,' said Louise. She held the flat of her hand over the top of her mineral water.

'I knew a man who drank Dog's Nose,' I said when I returned, suddenly madly euphoric, from the bar. 'He said it was like being hit on the temples simultaneously with two mallets. And you know what? It is!' Louise laughed politely and looked at her watch again. Did she really find this meeting so difficult that she wanted it to end already? Was I a disappointment to her? Perhaps she was waiting for the apology she undoubtedly deserved. I would have to take the plunge. 'I'm really sorry about that email,' I said. 'It was unforgivable. Of course I didn't mean it. I was in a state. I had spent the previous night on a park bench in Soho. Imagine – sleeping rough. I never thought I'd end up doing that. I felt terrible and I needed someone to blame.'

'I cried,' she said through tight lips. 'I was frightened.'

'Ahhh.' I put out a hand, which she pushed away.

'Still am,' she said. She looked again at her watch. I realized also that every time someone came through the door, Louise looked round. This wasn't going as I had expected.

'I'm really sorry,' I said. 'Are you expecting someone?'

She shook her head briefly. 'I just don't get it,' she said. 'What do you want?'

'Nothing. I thought you were into this too.'

'Into what? There is nothing to be into, that I can see.'

It was an impressive façade she was keeping up. I winked and repeated the telling phrase from her electronic invitation to meet in the Grapes. ' "It's in *Our Mutual Friend*." '

'I know,' replied Louise. 'It says so in the bar menu. What's that got to do with anything?'

'I thought you—.' I was beginning to feel foolish.

'Look, why don't you have another drink?' she said. 'You look like you need it. I'll get it. Have another whatsit.'

I stared at her figure standing at the bar. I saw two of her, twin Henriettas checking their watches simultaneously. I was confused as well as drunk, couldn't make any sense of the way the conversation had gone so far. She came back with another Dog's Nose. Nothing for her. 'You know,' I said, making one last attempt to show her the logic of our common ground. '*Our Mutual Friend*. The Six Jolly Fellowship Porters. Where we are.' I stabbed my finger down on the table. 'OK so far?'

'I think so.'

'Abbey Potterson, Muriel Belcher. Yes?'

'No. I don't know what you're talking about. I don't know you, and I don't want to know you. All I know is that you made me frightened and now—.' She glanced at the door and then at her watch.

I sighed. I struck my forehead with my thumbs. I drank off another couple of inches of Dog's Nose. Those town hall bells were beginning to chime. 'Well why the *fuck*,' I hit the table, hard enough for the glasses to rattle, and for conversations at adjacent tables to quieten momentarily, 'are you here?'

Louise looked at me with what I can only describe as hatred. 'Right,' she said. She began to gather her belongings together.

'No, please,' I urged her. I held out my hand but she recoiled. 'Stay. Let me explain. It's all Henrietta's fault. I thought she was you but she was a cunt instead.' I was aware that Louise was shaking her head but I pressed on. 'You have to see her. You have to see what I mean. Then you'll understand. Look.' I rummaged in my bag of books and papers. I found a newspaper obituary of Henrietta. 'She drank all day and her love life was uninhibited,' I read aloud. 'Here, look.' I pushed another newspaper cutting at Louise. It was about her funeral: 'Fifties Soho comes alive at funeral of a hell raiser.' I found the soft-porn Deakin shots, of Henrietta on the rumpled bed, and laid these out on the table where they darkened with spillage from my glass. In one she reclines on one side, her head against the back wall. On the bedside table is a stemmed glass half-full of clear liquid and a square glass ashtray with three or four butts in it. There is a post-coital languor about Henrietta in this shot. Her hair is ruffled, her eyes are cast demurely down, there are dark bags under her eyes. In the other picture, she sits forward smiling at the lens. Her breasts hang free. Her hands grasp her toes. Her lips are slightly parted. 'See?' I said. 'It's you. You to a T.'

'You're deluded,' she replied. At least I think that's what she said. I have to admit I was hardly listening by this point. I was ploughing on, which is unfortunate because otherwise I might have seen the signs and taken appropriate action – like getting the hell out of that pub. Instead, it all came out, as it can when you're drunk and excited. I told her about Josh, and the excavation I was carrying out on his time in Soho. I believe I even managed to weave in Karen, that long-ago girlfriend. I got sorry for myself. Josh, I said, had been all the things I wasn't: spontaneous, good at fighting, charismatic, irresistible to most women. I shot off at a tangent to hedge about this assertion with the kind of tedious qualifier that can suddenly assume vital importance when drunk: I said that *actually* it seemed he wasn't *quite* the person I had thought and wanted him to be – less assertive, rather docile etc. – but that, nevertheless and notwithstanding, broadly he was still a hero to me. So I envied him his attributes and his marvellous experiences, but more than that I envied the time and the place in which he was young. Soho in the fifties had been so much more – I sought the right words on the kippery ceiling – *innocent* and *vibrant* than our own tawdry times didn't she think? Would that we could walk through that door – I pointed to the pub entrance – and step back fifty years. Or alternatively, I added in a swoop of delight at my own ingenuity, given that we were also in the Fellowship Porters, would that we could step *forward* eighty years or so. The sight of the door now made me remember that I had been planning to go down to Booty's wine bar to see where Farson and perhaps Francis had lived. 'And here's something you don't know,' I said, forgetting that Louise had already told me she knew nothing. 'Here's something else you could have put in your email. Farson and Bacon both lived in Narrow Street, just a few doors down from here! Let's go and have a look.' I stood and grabbed her arm. She shook off my hand with a show of disgust which sobered me momentarily, reminding me of the look of stabbing hatred she had given me a few moments before when I had lost my temper. But I forgot this immediately in the headlong dive I was executing.

'No, I'll wait,' she said. 'But you go. You *will* come back, won't you?'

Confusing signals. My heart leapt at her apparent concern.

'I'll be back.' I left her with the table in front of her strewn with books and newspaper cuttings. I scooted out of that pub with a hop and a skip and sang my way down to Booty's a few doors along. A couple of construction workers in dusty boots, carrying yellow hard hats, stared at me as they passed.

The interior walls of Booty's were pebbledashed and painted the colour of Caucasian flesh. Maps of French wine regions had been affixed to the ceiling – you had to practically break your neck to read them – and there were red-and-white gingham cloths on the tables. Three people sat at the back, by the doors that opened on to the river terrace. Otherwise it was empty, with the forlorn air of a bar on its uppers. I tried, and failed, to imagine Bacon painting or drinking or mincing here. I came straight to the point with the barmaid, who had a bluebird tattoo next to an inoculation mark on her bare shoulder. 'Is it true that Francis Bacon lived here?' She looked at me blankly. 'You know, the painter. I think he lived here once.'

She continued to stare through me as she called out: 'John!'

A man wearing a green pinafore emerged from a room at the back holding a calculator. He looked me up and down.

'Is it true,' said the barmaid, 'that—. Who was it?'

'Francis Bacon,' I said.

'Lived here. This gentleman says he did.'

'Nah,' said John. 'Wassisname did though.'

'Dan Farson?' I said.

'That's it. And they were mates, like, him and Bacon. But Bacon never lived here, no.' I nodded, feeling foolish. I wanted to tell him that he was wrong but I had blown it. Having already asked whether Bacon had lived here, I could hardly answer my own question by averring that he did. 'All right?' said John as I stared at him. I nodded again. I wanted to help John and his dreary, empty, flesh-coloured bar. He could make something of the Bacon connection, have a few Bacon prints on the walls and information printed up on the back of the menus. Word would get round and earnest German art students would flock here. I said nothing, though, and after John had returned to the back room I felt obliged to order and despatch a drink – a small glass of Australian Chardonnay – before leaving.

Back in the Grapes, Louise seemed altogether more relaxed. She had put on fresh lipstick and tidied up my books and papers. 'Well that was a waste of time,' I said. I still had a Dog's Nose on the go and it was when I took a sip of it that I realized I wasn't very well. The gondola on my ferris wheel was beginning to sway, the bells were chiming again and the mallets swinging. I wasn't sure whether I wanted to be sick, or to succumb gloriously to diarrhoea. Perhaps both at the same time. I mumbled an apology and staggered up the narrow stairs to the Gents.

Two men followed me in. I'm hazy on what followed. It was a very small room and I think I just assumed at first there were too many of us in there together. Then I realized that there were hands on my shoulders, pulling me back, turning me round. I tried to yell, but one hand moved to my throat and the yell emerged as a gurgle. I was slammed against the wall. I saw four dusty building site boots shifting position with a strange unhurriedness on the floor; heard them scrape on the lino, the only sound but for three sets of laboured breathing. I scarcely saw the faces of the men, just the pursed lips and scrutinising frowns oddly reminiscent of, say, a watchmaker or silversmith at work. As my back hit the wall, one jabbed the nozzle of a soda siphon in my face and hit the handle with the meat of his thumb. I spluttered and gasped through the high-pressure jet of water. They weren't content to do my face. While one pinioned me to the wall the man with the siphon soaked me good and proper, from head to foot. The sound of the soda water escaping at speed reminded me of the day when, in Batty Langley's former house in Meard Street, I had heard the man urinating below and thought of Josh. This, at least, was how I took my mind off the fact of the most comprehensive physical humiliation I had ever undergone.

I'm not sure whether they had anything else in store for me after the soaking, for luckily someone else came into the Gents at this point, and my assailants relaxed their grip just long enough for me to get away. It sobered me up somewhat, I suppose. I remember clattering down the stairs back to the bar. I remember, as I pushed through the crowd, people flinching as my wet clothes came in contact with them. They must have been staring and laughing, but all I recall is Louise's face, those strong and symmetrical features effaced by what I took to be a look of blank horror. 'What happened?' she said.

And I replied, with imbecilic nonchalance, 'Oh nothing.'

'Oh nothing! Come on,' she said as I dripped water all over my papers and books and the photographic Henriettas turned into a sludge of newsprint. I told her what happened and she egged me on. The cunt, she egged me on. 'Who did it? Are they here, in the bar?' I said I hadn't seen them properly, but then I remembered the work boots. Through a thicket of legs I saw those boots, standing by the brass foot-rail that runs the length of the base of the bar. Their yellow hats were parked on the bar top. I pointed them out, but then I shrugged. What could I do? Big guys, two of them, off one of the Docklands building sites by the look of them. I couldn't take them on. I shrugged again. The evening had fallen to earth, left me in a puddle with a headache and without Louise, who plainly – and who could blame her – regarded me as a madman. I considered, with gloom, my journey back – all the way from East to West, then a car ride after that if I was sober enough. At least three hours of self-loathing before the oblivion of sleep. But then Louise said, 'What would Josh have done?'

I was so grateful she had remembered his name that I didn't see the elephant trap opening in front of me. 'Josh?' I said. 'He'd have taken them on of course.' And, momentarily forgetting my predicament, I told her, in excited detail, about the occasion when he had fought the two sailors as Bacon watched and waited.

'What are you waiting for?' she said.

'Josh was a trained boxer!' I protested. 'He did it in the navy.'

'Well,' was all she said. But she loaded the word with so much weariness and disappointment I knew I had to confound her. Before I could change my mind I picked up my pint of Dog's Nose, pushed through the crowd at the bar and poured what was left of the drink over one of the men who'd assaulted me with the soda siphon. It was just about the single stupidest thing I had ever done.

They didn't land any proper blows in the bar itself. We were quickly held apart by other drinkers, whereupon the manageress barred me on the grounds that I had started it by pouring my drink over the bloke's head. My protests were in vain. I called across the bar to Louise for corroboration, but suddenly, puzzlingly, she wasn't there. I gathered up my things in silence. Someone sniggered as I pushed my way out of the door. As the door banged to behind me, a cheer broke out, punctuated by shrieks of hysterical laughter. Out in Narrow Street I crossed to the far kerb and stood around, trying to collect my thoughts. The street seemed preternaturally quiet after the mayhem inside the Grapes; just a couple of parked cars, and the strange sense of contentment emanating from the biscuity Georgian brickwork. Where had Louise got to? I decided she must have gone to the Ladies at the decisive moment, that she would presently leave the pub. I no longer felt I had any chance with her but I needed to say something, make amends in some way. The door of the Grapes swung open presently and I started forward eagerly. But it wasn't Louise who came out. It was the men who had attacked me.

I didn't want to give them the satisfaction of seeing me run. Can you call that brave, when essentially it was a passive act? At any rate, I did not run. They beckoned me on but I simply stood my ground. They crossed the road, spreading out then moving back in as they approached me. I don't recall them saying anything, apart from 'Come on then.' They were curiously studious and joyless in their pursuit of violence. The first punch – to the stomach? the chin? I can't remember – took my legs away. The second or third kick, as I lay hunched on the pavement, sent me spiralling down a pitch-black well-shaft. I had a few quick and brightly coloured dreams, such as I remember having as a child after receiving a general anaesthetic at the dentist's. In one of these dreams, I was drinking in the Gargoyle with Raoul Walsh and he passed on some advice about film directing: 'You gotta remember kid. When in doubt, start a brawl.' In another dream, I was Josh, perched up on John Minton's roof in Apollo Place, watching Johnny's Circus cavorting below. Except that the dances of death and love I watched through the skylights were not being played out by Minton's acolytes but by more familiar faces: a cloaked and cadaverous De Quincey hunting for Ann, who cowered in a room De Quincey was destined never to enter; Farson running after Josh; Josh after Henrietta; me after Louise. Me after Josh: seeing him in the French and running up behind him, clapping him on the shoulder and shouting his name; and him looking straight through me, as if one of us wasn't there.

When I regained consciousness the first thing I saw were four feet. Two people were standing over me, and when I looked up I saw that one of them was Louise. The owner of the other pair of feet drew back his leg as if to kick me, and as I flinched I heard Louise say, 'Don't. He's had enough.'

The other person said to me: 'You got what you deserved. Perhaps that'll teach you to stop harassing my wife.'

I struggled into a sitting position and peered upward. This person seemed horribly familiar. As my eyes focused on his thick-rimmed, tinted specs, I saw he was the property editor at the newspaper I worked for. Liking for lettuce. He had his arm round Louise. 'Your *wife*?' I kept repeating this question.

JOSH AVERY BY UNKNOWN STUDIO PHOTOGRAPHER

Chapter 12

By the time the armoured van containing the disgraced naval rating, Michael Joseph Avery, passed between the blue cast-iron gates of the Royal Navy Detention Quarters in Portsmouth, Josh's two black eyes had passed the acme of luridness but his tongue was still exploring an unfamiliar oral terrain created by the loss of two more teeth. After the coppers had roughed him up in London, he had been duffed over in the cells in Portsmouth as he awaited the court martial in which he received a ninety-day sentence in DQs, as it was known, to be followed by dismissal from the service. When the van stopped in the courtyard of DQs and the rear doors were flung open Josh was obliged, with a fellow reprobate whose offence had been to get blind drunk at the Royal Tournament, to sprint into the detention block. From now on, just about every public activity had to be conducted 'at the double'. After presenting his razor for inspection every morning – to check he hadn't taken the blade out in order to kill himself with it later – Josh was obliged to sprint down from his cell to collect his breakfast of porridge; to sprint down to the latrine with his toilet bucket, its contents slopping on his plimsolls; to run while square bashing, with the added requirement of holding a rifle out in front and at shoulder height as he marched; to run for his lunch of macaroni and boiled fish and to run for his tea of bread and jam.

This was pretty much what he had expected and he coped with it well enough, he said. It was the ruinously pointless 'duties' they forced him to carry out which really ate away at his soul. Whitewashing coal. Digging a hole and filling it up again. Cutting the grass with nail scissors. Plaiting strands of hemp into rope; above all, this. Even after so many years, he remembered it clearly: forty-two strands of hemp, each eighteen inches long, had to be plaited together and pulled to an exacting torque, with bare fingers and no instruments, to create a thick cord of rope. The effect of working the coarse strands was akin to sticking your fingers in an extractor fan with razor-sharp blades. Sitting on the tea chest, Josh had leant forward to show me the scars. His finger tips were flattened and corrugated (he made a joke about how he would have made a good burglar on account of having no finger prints). It was a humiliation too far. On most aspects of his life, as I've said, he was phlegmatic. He told me that if Dan Farson walked through the cottage door there and then he would have harboured no hard feelings despite strongly suspecting, though he had never been able to prove it, that it was Farson who tipped off the police that a naval deserter was on the run and where to find him. As Josh pointed out, people were capable of terrible things without being all bad themselves, and that little apophthegm applied to no one more aptly than to Josh himself. But he could not find it in him to forgive the Navy for his experiences in DQs and got very worked up talking about them. Some might say he got what was coming to him, but I don't think it was as simple as that.

It was paint that got us on to the subject of what happened after he was arrested and court martialled. In the room where we passed the evenings in the cottage the plaster had been removed from the walls while the timber beneath was treated for wet and dry rot. What colour, I asked Josh, gesturing at those forlornly denuded walls, should I paint the room, did he think? I had been thinking of a plain white, but perhaps that was a boring option, a lost opportunity. Perhaps I should go with the natural darkness and snugness of the room and choose a dark colour? He recommended to me the National Trust range of 'authentic' paints, which later I would notice gathered in clusters of tins in the basement of Batty Langley's house in Meard Street. He told me he had recently completed the painting of a posh house in the Downs behind Brighton. The woman of the house had driven him to distraction by changing her mind umpteen times, depending on what interior or style magazines she had been reading, about what colours she wanted. Her choice of colour for the main room, for instance, had moved from brilliant white to gardenia and then terracotta before she had settled on dead salmon. Josh said he had offered no opinion at any stage, knowing from bitter experience that that way trouble lay, that by keeping out of it he could never be blamed. He said the same to me. He told me the only colour he would ever comment on – and that in the negative – was that shade of rather sickly off-white favoured by jerry-builders and council painters known as magnolia. He drew the line at magnolia – could recognize this hateful hue from a hundred paces and refused to dip his brush in it – for no better reason than that magnolia had been the colour of his cell in DQs. It wasn't the colour itself, or even the memories it triggered, which offended him so. It was because one of the screws had made a point of explaining to him – had taken pleasure, indeed, in telling him – that the colour of the walls had been chosen by a psychologist because it was supposed to have a calming effect on inmates. Concrete, when camouflaged in magnolia paint, was reckoned by some head doctor to be as soothing as a lullaby.

The idea of this had enraged Josh. It wasn't the cramped dimensions – six feet by ten feet – of the cell, the wafer thin, stained mattress, the horse-hair blankets or the stinking toilet bucket, which pushed Josh over the edge. He had coped with such things and worse in the orphanage, aboard ship and in his homeless Soho days. It was the expectation that he would be calmed by paint, that he would be good as gold on account of a certain emulsion. The several occasions on which he went berserk – as virtually nothing was smashable, this consisted of yelling a great deal and chucking the contents of his toilet bucket around, preferably over a screw if one was foolish enough to venture inside his cell – each earned him a three-day stint in solitary confinement. And it was here, in solitary, that Josh reached the pitch-dark, oxygen-starved bottom of the well; the place in which he could not conceive of there being a way back up.

The bitterness, as I've said, stayed with him. Most people who knew Josh in his later life knew from personal experience his potential for violence. My friend Dave, Josh's stepson, for instance, related to me several stories in which Josh got drunk and disgraced himself, either by threatening or perpetrating violence. In one memorable incident in 1980, he got very exercised by a weekend guest at Greensands who presumed to praise the SAS for the manner in which they had just concluded the Iranian Embassy siege. Jean, Josh and some friends – of whom the SAS fancier was one – were sitting drinking on the terrace when this person, very smirky after a sherry or two, said he felt he could now sleep safer in his bed as a result of the actions of the brave men in balaclavas. Josh, who was drinking cider at the time on the grounds that it was little more than apple juice, snapped at this inane comment, and proceeded to ruin what had been shaping up into a rather idyllic, lazy summer's day in the country by punching the man out and then toppling over backwards into the pond, scattering the geese. Many such stories I had heard of Josh's explosions of drunken rage and how they had ruined parties or weekends or those holidays in Spain that Jean and Josh went on for several consecutive years in the late seventies. I am grateful that I never witnessed him get near to this level of aggression – except once; and that occasion was in my cottage when he talked of DQs. When the subject of solitary came up, I saw the violent anger flare in his eyes and tauten in his fists as I had never seen it before.

In solitary – in the dark, in his PE shorts and vest, on a concrete platform, for three days solid – he had time, for the first time, to reflect upon his summer in Soho. And already it seemed distant and unreal. It had been no more than a trespass, he decided. He had found himself by the wall, and he had managed to shin up and over the wall and romp undetected on the other side. And now he had been caught and returned to the outside, where he was being punished for his presumption in scaling that wall. For what went on in Soho – all that loving and drinking and betrayal – wasn't for the likes of him. While Farson wept into another sailor's neck, and Henrietta, bumming another brandy off Norman, enquired casually, 'Seen Mick lately? Whatever happened to him?', Josh numbed his arse on concrete and corroded his soul with bitterness in a Portsmouth cell. He never really got over that sense of being punished for somehow overstepping the mark, presuming to take a bigger slice of life than his birthright allowed. It explained, too, his great and abiding sorrow in not being an artist of some sort, for art is its own aristocracy, artistic talent is the ladder that gets otherwise unsuitable people up and over the wall. In the future any bourgeois prick who reminded him, however inadvertently, that he was no more than a hick without accomplishments, anyone who laughed at him or wanted to fuck him, but wasn't prepared to help him, was liable to end up on their knees hunting for teeth. This was Josh's revenge for the sweetness he lost forever in Soho, and the realization of that loss that he came to in solitary confinement in naval DQs.

After ninety days, at seven o'clock on a freezing February morning, he was released. He had just a few bob and a train voucher in his pocket, and his finger ends, ribbed and spatulate, were practically devoid of feeling. Breathing the salty freedom of Pompey, he walked to the London road and stuck out his disfigured thumb. Back in Soho, he found himself invisible. He stood and waited in Meard Street until they came, one by one. Henrietta passed with a baby, singing *Bye Bye Blackbird* to the little mite, so engrossed she didn't notice the man who had once urinated on her. Farson had eyes only for a new sailor he had in tow. Bacon frowned momentarily as his eyes flickered across Josh's motionless figure before he danced on with an explosion of gaiety directed at his musclebound, sharply-suited companion. There was an inexhaustible supply of handsome, eager young men to feed the furnace of Soho. Their hair might not be as luxuriant as Josh's, but their noses might be more aquiline. They might not inspire a Bacon painting, but they would sleep with Farson as well as Henrietta. Josh was dispensible, interchangeable. Invisible, or dead, was how he felt as he stood unacknowledged in the shadows of Meard Street watching the happy-hour heel-clackers. In the time it took to mutilate his finger tips in a concrete cell, the mark he had made on the Soho myth had already faded to illegibility.

He could have had Farson for shopping him – did in fact contemplate jumping the blond, blubbery one as he passed oblivious by – but he decided to keep his nose clean. It was time to move on, and that meant Hampstead. But the Empsons' house was locked and deserted. He waited a day and a night but no one returned. In time he would move in with Hetta and William Empson, and over twelve years this arrangement would evolve into the classic French triangle. By way of rent he slept with Hetta and, on William's returns from Sheffield, he slept, or at least would share a bed, with

William and allow the author of *Seven Types of Ambiguity* and *Milton's God* to rub himself off against the small of his back. But for now the Empsons were away so he turned to Frank. He went to the Rosslyn Arms and waited until Frank came in. Frank arrived in tears. 'Look,' he said. He produced from his pocket two pieces of an onyx ring. 'My wedding ring, broken. It's a bad omen.'

Frank had got engaged to a German girl while Josh had been in DQs. One night, before Josh's arrest, Frank and Josh had fought over this girl. Josh had sent her home from the pub one night because Frank was ignoring her. When Frank returned from the Gents to discover that Josh had suggested to her that she should go, for the sake of her dignity, he was furious. The girl was very good in bed, he told me, and he always looked forward to taking her home with him after closing time. He took Josh outside and hit him. Josh did not hit him back but simply said, 'That's all right.' Sitting in the pub garden in Steyning where I fed him drinks, Frank had roared with laughter as he told this story.

'You're *marrying* her?' said Josh, gazing at the pieces of broken ring that Frank held up.

'I'm marrying her,' confirmed Frank. 'You been somewhere, by the way? I haven't seen you around for ages ...' Frank drank until the broken ring seemed unimportant. 'I need a fling,' he said, 'before getting wed. A final fling. The condemned man's breakfast. Let's go somewhere.'

'Monte Carlo,' said Josh. 'The palm trees, the sea.'

'Monte Carlo? That's not for us.' He fingered the frayed lapels of Josh's jacket. 'We'd be chewing-gum on their boot soles, my son. We could do Spain, though. Spain's good. Lots of sea and palm trees. Wine for a bob a flagon.'

'*Señoritas*,' said Josh.

'*Maracas*,' said Frank.

'*Olé*,' said Josh.

Frank and Josh took the boat to Bilbao in northern Spain. During the sailing they befriended a district nurse from the New Forest called Nora. Nora had her car with her and was intending to drive to Morocco to visit the grave of her son, who'd been killed in a road accident there. They cadged a lift from Nora as far as Madrid, where they met an Englishman called Bill in a bar. After giving Nora a liquid send-off they returned to Bill's fifth-floor apartment where they continued to get roaring drunk, and Bill cut himself badly on a broken glass. Losing large quantities of blood, Bill then decided it would be amusing or dramatic to climb out on to the narrow stone lintel beyond the windows of his apartment. Here he had squatted, not quite confident enough to stand entirely upright, while Josh and Frank applauded from inside, and a growing crowd of people gathered below, dodging the blood which fell among them in drops the size of sultry rain. 'I can see him now,' said Frank fondly, 'the mad cunt, hollering like a pig. The whole of Madrid was stood down there watching him.'

'But what was he doing it for?' I asked.

And Frank had looked at me strangely. 'It was just the days they were,' he said. 'Or the age we were. Or both. You didn't do things for a reason. You did things for no reason. There's too much reason around these days. Like this glass.' He lifted the latest vodka and tonic I had bought him. 'Reason says I shouldn't drink this. Well ...' And Frank lit another cig.

When the police arrived, Frank tried to prevent them entering the apartment and ended up hitting one of them. While Bill was taken to hospital, Frank and Josh were arrested and put in the back of a police car. During the journey to the station, Josh unzipped himself and urinated on the backs of the heads of the policemen in the front seats. The police stopped the car, hauled Josh out and stripped him naked. They then used his clothes to towel their heads and mop up the urine. Frank was unclear about what happened at the police station. He supposed they had been beaten up and slung in cells, but the next thing he could remember was the police dropping them off beyond the city boundary, booting them from the vehicle with a *Hijos de puta!* They had then hitchhiked south in a succession of jalopies, sleeping in fields, getting diarrhoea on a diet of fruit and, in Josh's case, trying to befriend the many stray dogs they encountered.

In Marbella, then just a fishing village, Frank came moderately to his senses. They were on the beach and Josh was suggesting they offer to help the fishermen unload the catch every mid morning in return for a few fish themselves. It was still only April and they could expect to live like that until at least October, said Josh, sleeping on the beach and cooking supper on fires. Frank pointed out that he had a wedding to return for. He looked at Josh properly for the first time. Josh still wore the clothes that had been used to mop up his urine. His hair was matted, he had a thick, unkempt beard, his limbs were skeletally thin from lack of proper food, he had lesions on his neck that were presumably also to do with poor diet. 'He'd aged about twenny years,' said Frank. 'And I thought: "If *he* looks bad then so must I." I thought: "This is madness, we don't have to be doing this." I said to him: "Mike, we don't have to be doing this. I've still got a bit of money, and I can always wire to Beate for some more. We can have a few days in a decent pension in the village, sink some vino, then think about getting back. What do you say? I get married in a fortnight."' Frank took a slug of vodka, shrugged. 'Didn't wanna know. Not interested. He just said, "Go ahead, do what you like, I'm staying here." So I did. I booked myself into a hotel, smartened myself up and just about got back in time for the wedding. It didn't last more than five minutes, but that's another story. But you know what, I think he was happy on that beach. The last time I saw him, until he turned up at Hetta's about six months later with his leg in plaster, he was sitting on a dune surrounded by stray dogs. He used to pick up the fish guts and feed 'em to 'em. Happy as Larry. Stank like a fish factory, mind you.'

For a year or more after Josh painted the cottage I was finding the remains of his rolies littered about the garden. Stiffened by the sun or sodden by rain, with strands of tobacco trailing from the flattened fragments of paper tube, they seemed surprisingly durable and I looked forward to coming upon them for several years to come. They were comforting relics of his life, like finding a half-eaten slice of toast in a kitchen and making the reasonable assumption that someone had just popped out in mid breakfast and would shortly be back. Josh was only ever between cigarettes now, and one day I would turn a corner in the garden and there would be not just a discarded butt, but the man himself, still smoking it. But then I stopped finding the butts. I took to poking about in the undergrowth with a stick, hoping to turn one up. Nothing. I told myself this was no bad thing. It simply meant that now, finally, was the time to come to terms with the fact that Josh was well and truly dead. This hankering after the past, this morbid identification with a dead person, was not healthy. But I did not find these thoughts comforting.

After what happened in the Grapes, I returned to the cottage in a state of shock and mooched about for days in a haze. The bottle of wine in the fridge, the two glasses I had polished and put out on the table on the mad assumption that Louise would return with me to the cottage, mocked me so mercilessly I smashed them. I started, and abandoned, several emails to both my editor and to his wife. His wife! My jaw had swelled so much from being kicked in the head that I couldn't eat properly for days and survived on tinned soup. I remembered Josh's cigarette butts and went on some fruitless searches for them. I paused often in front of the burnmark on the window ledge that I had painted around. I sat out in the garden, where we had sat together on that limpid summer's evening when he had pointed out the browning of the leaves in the uppermost branches of the beech trees, and I had felt a chill of premonition. I turned sideways, gazing at the space he had occupied, imagining the wrinkles that fanned from the corners of his eyes. 'Tell me more about Bacon,' I wanted to say. 'Tell me more about Cecilia. I liked her. Oh, and by the way I found her! She's still around, living in Sloane Street.' But there was nothing, no one to talk to.

All those books that gave you the wrong idea about Soho. Well, Jean and Josh – unwittingly, through the weekends at Greensands they invited me on – had misled me about living in the country. I had imagined a kind of perpetual, lazy summer of Pimm's on the tongue and bees on the stamen. Distant horses neighed as we dozed through the afternoons. The geese, like schoolmasters Dave and I had known, were both self-important and of no importance. A chevron of golden light on my knee, and then Test Match Special, turned down, followed by the discreet popping of corks. But at my cottage it was always windy and wet, and no one came, just the rabbits, fat and insatiable, and, in the pre-dawn, the white-arsed roe deer who ate the flowers and shrubs. Inside, despite the traps and poisons I deployed, the mice were proliferating, and the insufferable smell of mingled mouse urine and decomposing mouse flesh made me gag. It did not take me long to decide: I would sell up; nose back into the great metropolitan swell of things and people; try living in this new century for a change. But first I would do what I should have done several months ago, when the warning signs were there and I chose to ignore them. I would take a holiday.

It wasn't all to be chilling out, though. I reckoned I just might have one last throw of the dice as far as my editor was concerned. At our last lunch he had made that rather off-the-cuff suggestion about English criminals' gaffs on the Costa del Sol. It would be a laugh, he suggested, to find one or two: meet the hoods with medallions and perms and rottweilers, snoop round their circular beds and guitar-shaped swimming pools, knock back their antifreeze-coloured cocktails, note carefully the connubially conjugated villa names: Davellen, Tracelee. Now *that*, he had said, was a sexy property story – and a short-cut to the mortuary, I had thought at the time. But now I had little to lose and if villains' villas turned him on, that's what I'd endeavour to give him.

I booked a short break; flew to Malaga, where a bus transferred me to my resort hotel in Marbella. That first evening I strolled along the *ésplanade*, past the private villas, until the bass thump of music faded and all I heard was the waves, gaining the beach in short, hissing rushes followed by long exhalations of undertow. Presently the path rounded a headland and joined the corniche where it formed a pavement on the seaward side and I shared my walk with the occasional speeding convertible. A soft, greenish dusk had settled. Out to sea, towards Africa, the lights of fishing boats shone suddenly bright in the gauzy light. I honestly wasn't thinking about him but then there he was, on the beach, in the shade of a palm tree whose fronds creaked faintly in the merest offshore breeze. One dog lay in a spiral of sleeping fur at his feet. Another, its back legs splayed at ten to two, slurped greedily on its private parts. Josh was barefoot, emaciated, his beard was full and black, like McCartney's at the time of *Let It Be*. I was just wondering how to address him, mindful of how I had blown it in the French that time, when he raised his arm and grinned, in a 'what kept you?' sort of way.